Sumptuous Dining

IN GASLIGHT SAN FRANCISCO

1875-1915

Sumptuous Dining

IN GASLIGHT SAN FRANCISCO

1875–1915

FRANCES DE TALAVERA BERGER
&
JOHN PARKE CUSTIS

DOUBLEDAY & COMPANY, INC., GARDEN CITY, NEW YORK   1985

Library of Congress Cataloging in Publication Data

Berger, Frances de Talavera, 1931–
    Sumptuous dining in gaslight San Francisco (1875–1915)

    Includes index.
    1. Cookery, American—California.   2. San Francisco
(Calif.)—Social life and customs.   3. San Francisco
(Calif.)—Restaurants—History.   I. Custis, John Parke,
1930–   II. Title.
TX715.B4827 1985   641.5′09794′61   83-45372
ISBN 0-385-19252-5

Designed by Judith Neuman

First Edition

CONTENTS

V.

HOWEVER, NOT ALL THE GREAT COOKS WERE MEN

VI.

Sound, sound the clarion, fill the fife!
Throughout the sensual world proclaim,
One crowded hour of glorious life
Is worth an age without a name.

. . . THOMAS OSBERT MORDAUNT

AUTHOR'S NOTE

While most of the recipes in this collection may be confidently followed or comfortably adapted to modern cooking, and, indeed, the authors have substituted present-day ingredients whenever possible to replace the vague or the archaic in the original, there are a few recipes which were included precisely because they are precious curio pieces. In such cases, we have made a sincere attempt to point out to the reader that the particular recipe is, above all, primarily of historic value. However, whenever possible, we have also adjusted the ingredients or the cooking methods of these rare pieces to accommodate the contemporary cook. Also, these recipes might contain some variance in the serving portions; conscientious care has been given this feature in order to please the taste of the more fastidious modern palate. Still, the reader is urged to try them, and, most important of all for the enjoyment of exotic cooking, to heartily experiment.

INTRODUCTION
TO A GOLDEN ERA

ADMITTEDLY, WE SAN FRANCISCANS ARE A HOPELESSLY CHAUVINISTIC LOT. Entrusted with a city that has been lovingly fashioned over the years with wit, whimsy, and unabashed wealth into an exclusive, stately pleasure dome, we fully intend to keep it that way. Nor is the native the only incurable addict; the visitor, both casual or sophisticated, easily succumbs to "everybody's favorite city."

If all the ink used to print the purple prose describing San Francisco's lifestyle were suddenly spilled, no doubt it would cover the earth. Perhaps Lucius Beebe described it best: "Everything about San Francisco smells deliciously of money or Sauce Mornay!" From his self-imposed exile in New York, the notorious gadfly of Eastern café society, C. V. R. Thompson, fired back a volley of pure jealousy. "I never see Mr. Beebe without being reminded of aging red plush, polished mahogany, and faded satin. To me, he looks like an exhibit that has been brought back to life." Intentional or otherwise, San Francisco graciously accepted Mr. Thompson's backhanded accolade. But it was left to an Easterner, Willie Britt, to put it in exact perspective. "I'd rather be a busted lamp post on Battery Street in San Francisco than the Waldorf-Astoria!" Over the ages, the adoring prose dedicated to *bon vivant* San Francisco runs the gamut from an obscure historian of the 1850s who noted: "No people in the world live faster or more sumptuously than the people of San Francisco," to our own Herb Caen, who has definitively christened it "Baghdad-by-the-Bay."

Great cities tend to keep their original characters, regardless of age. In our own country, where modernity is a fact of life, the great cities still manage to mix elements of their pasts with their present ambiance. Perhaps in no other way is a city's finesse and worth better measured than by its continuing meticulous attention to the sensual art of food, cooking, and restaurants. New York spawned the best restaurants in the United States because it maintained a healthy respect for the magnificent cuisine of its polyglot citizenry. Regrettably,

I

that city's eating habits are declining scandalously, thanks to an easy seduction by its own media blitz for compulsive consumption and the restaurants' obscene, hilariously high prices. Chicago began as a friendly, robust, hearty beef-eating town, and, quaintly, nothing much has changed. New Orleans was blessed from birth with a great style of cuisine and, it is hoped, will recover from its current identity crisis: French, Creole, Cajun, or junk food? Los Angeles is a quixotic exception. Once shackled with a bizarre image as a sleepy little pueblo where the only excitement it ever experienced was the inevitable debris slopping into the sea, California's most hedonistic city now rivals New York as the dynamic culinary center of the United States.

How does San Francisco view this gastronomic brouhaha? The best way to describe it is complacently, because it experienced this culinary upheaval very early in its career. Once freed of its boring burden of being a foreign *Presidio,* the city quickly became a ·noisy, bawdy, naughty prostitute during the Gold Rush of 1849 and then effortlessly progressed to the grand stance of a refined courtesan by the time the Palace Hotel opened its opulent dining room in 1875. Despite the debilitating and almost fatal fits of despicable civic consciousness, the infamous eating and drinking debaucheries of the Barbary Coast continued unabated until put to a final death by the Clubwomen's Vigilance Committee in 1921. But San Franciscans fondly preserve memories of a checkered past, culinary or otherwise, and we use that general nostalgia as the foundation for our present municipal pride. In fact, this old ballad might be the anthem of our very civilized city:

> *The miners came in forty-nine,*
> *The whores in fifty-one;*
> *And when they got together,*
> *They produced the native son!*

With such a roguish past, it is small wonder nothing can surprise a San Franciscan. And with such a heritage, combined with the Westerner's marvelous sense of humor, it is hardly necessary to confess we have remained somewhat mildly wicked. What we have successfully accomplished, from a tumultuous beginning to the controversial present, is to raise defiantly the art of city living to its highest level. And the art of living must include among its prerequisites a lusty passion for fine dining.

A self-avowed "Californiac," Inez Haynes rhapsodized over San Francisco as a place where "Spring comes in the fall and the fall comes in the summer and the summer comes in the winter—and the winter never comes at all!" We leave it to the poets to suggest that the very forces of nature—the cool winds, the fogs, the pure air—unerringly combine around the city to spur the native and tourist alike to seek the delights of great dining. In the early 1900s, Marie Weiss, a lifelong San Franciscan, wrote an eloquent, heartfelt poem that seems to capture the special lure of San Francisco for both the natives and the visitors:

> *Beautiful city with lights aglow,*
> *From the crest of your hills to the waters below,*
> *A garden festooned with lanterns bright,*
> *Shining afar like stars of night.*

> *Land of sunshine, of mirth and cheer,*
> *Your smile is genial 'tis good to be here.*
> *A dear personality, distinctly your own.*
> *Land of Bohemia and home, sweet home!*

I.

THE EPICUREAN SENSUALISTS WHO MADE IT HAPPEN

IN 1897, IT WAS RUMORED THAT AT LEAST A HUNDRED THOUSAND RESIDENTS of San Francisco were outright public nuisances. In no other city but ours would the citizens have laughed at that gross figure. Between the nuisances and the nabobs, it is safe to say that half the population must have functioned, if it functioned at all, only during the night. Since the San Francisco sun is infamous for being elusive, it is questionable how many citizens ever saw the sun at all during those halcyon years.

Ned Greenway, the rotund social arbiter and promoter of society's fanciest cotillions, never rose before four o'clock in the afternoon. In those palmy days, the very poor and the very rich shared a unique circumstance; both groups were known collectively as the "Very Late at Night Set." The cocktail hour was their breakfast time, and late supper at three o'clock in the morning signaled the end of a typically decadent evening. They lived in swirling fogs and perpetual darkness; the only light that punctuated their lives was the glow of gaslight. William H. Chambliss, Nob Hill's venomous spark plug, wrote that, because such a large segment of the population was almost always intoxicated, the people could no longer tell the difference between the night and the day. He may have been only slightly exaggerating. In the 1890s, San Francisco had one authorized saloon for every ninety-six inhabitants, not counting the more than two thousand speakeasies insidiously operating without licenses.

From the mist of this besotted milieu, six epicureans arose to set a new standard for eating and drinking for our robust town. They made their presence strongly felt in the late 1890s. By that time, San Francisco had recovered from its "fried egg" complex, and society's darlings had learned to say, "*Très sec*, please!" when they requested French Pommery wine. The notorious six were a mixed but ideal lot: a superior restaurateur; a brawling, hard-drinking street reporter and poet; a sophisticate who was a successful merchant; a hotel man-

ager at the very peak of his profession; an amateur cook and a general
man-about-town; and, finally, one of the greatest chefs to wash up
on this or any other shore. With the ecstatic cooperation of all the
classes, from the "Dead Slow Set" to the "Nice People," these six
gourmets inspired the Bay City to live up to its reputation as "the
finest jewel on the brow of the night."

The sensual six firmly set out on their sacred mission to raise the
town above the horror of rank barbarism, and they very defiantly
ignored the many pressures heaped upon them by the various social
cliques holding sway at the time. The "Conservative Set," as might
be expected, did not approve of them; the six ignored this nest of
high teas and ossified chastity. The "Fast Set" was barely tolerated
by our classy sextet. In spirit, our *bon vivants* were closest to the
"Smart Set," which had been wickedly dubbed the "Irish Push" by
its detractors. With the majority of the population cheering them
on, the six epicureans gleefully scorned the hypocritical matrons of
Nob Hill who blatantly bought titled princes as gifts for their submis-
sive, weak-kneed daughters, threatening to turn San Francisco into
a transplanted Ruritania. As for Ned Greenway and his refined cotillions, the cultured six ribaldly suggested that if his debutantes were
the toast of the town, then, most assuredly, roly-poly Greenway was
the butter. The epicureans agreed that, Greenway's social pretensions
notwithstanding, his father probably plucked turkeys somewhere in
North Dakota.

Consternation was considerable in the highest society when the
spiteful William H. Chambliss took up his pen and cruelly wrote,
"The ladies of Oakland look much healthier and brighter than their
counterparts in San Francisco. Could it be that they keep better
hours?" The pious Chambliss also raised his voice against the suffragette Laura De Force Gordon, who was fighting for the right of
San Francisco's women to ride bicycles wearing bloomers. Surprisingly, she eventually won her case. In the same year, the fancier
ladies of the evening, ensconced in elegant *maisons de joie*, experienced
a tremendous boom in business. Certainly they seemed content to
stay indoors. Here was an issue, however, that the suffragette and
the pious writer could agree on, but neither Miss Gordon's constant
blandishments nor Mr. Chambliss' shrill scoldings could coax these
belles to exercise in the fresh air.

What the city's prostitutes *did* relish, instead, was the stupendous
success of one of their cohorts. She had married a senator's son, and

they had gone on a grand honeymoon across Europe. Why shouldn't her former counterparts sigh and dream and hope that fate would be as kind to them? After all, she had climbed the nearly insurmountable mountain of high society. Ah, yes, San Francisco was beginning to change since the decades following the Gold Rush, when the lusty population idolized and patronized such female "artistes" affectionately known as "The Little Lost Chicken," "The Galloping Cow," "The Waddling Duck," "The Roaring Gimlet," "The Dancing Heifer," and "Lady Jane Grey"!

The writer Frank Norris said, "San Francisco is a city where almost anything can happen." This did not surprise the six pace-setting sensualists. Of course, they noted the unexpected and shocking death at sea of Dolly Adams, the notorious "Water Queen of Ellis Street," with considerable relief: The "Water Queen" might well have blown the whistle on the secret pleasures of many of their closest friends who also trod heavily on the ambrosial path. In the years after the Great Fire, the famous "Queen of the Underworld," the wondrously diamond-bedecked Bessie Hall Ladeau, reigned supreme from another Ellis Street address. Bessie Hall had learned to keep her mouth shut and was greatly admired by her patrons because she was never known to have "kissed and told." If ever our six conspirators experienced a severe shock, it might have been the evening when the luscious May Brookyn, an "actress" of the melodramatic stage, appeared suddenly at Marchand's elegant restaurant and tragically swallowed poison. The young girl, victim of an unrequited grand passion for a gentleman of very high station, then proceeded to drop dead in front of the horrified patrons.

San Francisco was now wrapping itself deliciously in fashionable Paris gowns and sparkling diamonds, while its "gentlemen" imbibed the very best French champagne, imported brandies, and the most expensive caviar money could buy. For the six epicurean sensualists who made it all happen, Edward Lytton, writing as "Owen Meredith," summed it up most beautifully:

> *We may live without poetry, music and art;*
> *We may live without conscience, and live without heart;*
> *We may live without friends; we may live without books;*
> *But civilized man cannot live without cooks.*

EDWARD BLANQUIE, the extraordinary restaurateur
Photo courtesy of the California Section, California State Library

Edward Blanquie
The Restaurateur Extraordinaire

There has been a Jack's Restaurant in San Francisco since 1864. Jacques Monique, who bought the establishment in 1884, originally called it Jack's Rotisserie. As the century closed, this "Jack" sold out to Edward Blanquie, who became the quintessential restaurateur of the period. His culinary contributions are still revered. The current Jack's Restaurant is situated at 615 Sacramento Street, and many of Blanquie's original dishes have remained on the menu. If Blanquie had not resisted a name-change when he purchased the premises, he would not have been mistaken frequently for Jacques Monique, or even more often for Antoine de Bua Blanco, the distinguished proprietor of Blanco's Restaurant, which opened in 1907. Both Blanco and Blanquie began their respective culinary careers in San Francisco by offering the finest quality foodstuffs available, but, for the most part, only Blanquie's special recipes have survived. For this, and for making the business of cooking a fine art, he deserves to be honored.

During the last years of the nineteenth century, only a handful of restaurants had reputations as "the best." Unfortunately, nearly all perished in the Great Fire of 1906. They included Marchand's, the favorite of Sarah Bernhardt; the elegant Maison Riche, at the corner of Geary and Grant streets, owned by Justin Ladagnous and John Somali; the Maison Doree, noted for its oysters and frog legs; Delmonico's, on O'Farrell Street, with its discreet, naughty side carriage entrance; the Old Poodle Dog, known as the most expensive of them all; and the Pup, at Stockton and Market streets, where Chef Pierre personally cooked his famous fish in wine sauce.

Jack's was not among this early select group; its turn was to come. During Blanquie's tenure, the restaurant was noted for Jack's Roman Punch, a blend of semisoft ice cream with rum or other liquors folded into its creamy consistency. The punch was served as a mid-dinner refreshment or pleasant dessert. Also universally popular in San Francisco, and a specialty of Jack's, was this old-fashioned delicacy:

TRIPES *à la Mode de Caen*

> 4 pounds fresh honeycomb tripe
> 4 calves' feet
> 1 onion
> 2 cups chopped celery
> 6 carrots
> 2 cups dry white wine
> Salt and pepper to taste
> 2 bay leaves
> 2 teaspoons dried marjoram
> 3 teaspoons dried parsley
> 2 teaspoons dried thyme
> ½ teaspoon salt
> 4 ounces calvados or cognac

Wash the tripe, trim it, and soak it overnight. Drain. Preheat the oven to 250 degrees F. Immerse the tripe in fresh water, bring it to a boil in a separate skillet, and then drain it. Cut it into small strips and, in a large clay pot or heavy casserole, combine the tripe with the rest of the ingredients—except 3 of the carrots—and the calvados or cognac. Cover the pot very tightly; bake the tripe for 8 hours. Then remove and discard the vegetables; remove and set aside the calves' feet. Bake the tripe for another 4 hours at the same temperature. If the liquid has become low, add more wine. One hour before it is finished, add the remaining 3 carrots, sliced, to the pot. Cut the meat from the calves' feet; shortly before serving, thoroughly mix the meat and the calvados or cognac with the tripe. Serve the dish warm. SERVES 8 AS AN ENTRÉE.

Equally elegant, but less dependent on a classically trained palate, are these recipes by Blanquie:

MUSHROOMS *à la Edward*

> 12 large mushrooms
> 2 tablespoons imported olive oil
> Freshly ground black pepper to taste
> Salt to taste
> Mushrooms à la Edward Sauce

Remove the stems from the mushrooms and reserve for sauce. Wash and dry the mushrooms, arrange them in a single layer, and dress them with imported olive oil, ground black pepper, and a little salt. Let them stand for 1 hour. Preheat the broiler. Drain the mushrooms and broil them. Pour the sauce over the mushrooms and serve them immediately. SERVES 6 AS AN APPETIZER.

MUSHROOMS *à la Edward* Sauce

> 12 mushroom stems
> Chicken broth to cover
> Fresh parsley, minced, to taste
> ½ cube butter
> Juice of 1 lemon
> ¼ cup heavy cream
> Dash of arrowroot

Wash, dry, and mince the mushroom stems. Put them in a skillet with enough chicken broth to cover them, minced parsley to the cook's touch, the butter, and lemon juice. Over low heat, add the cream and thicken the sauce slightly with arrowroot, stirring constantly.

BLANQUIE'S FILLETS OF SOLE IN WINE

> 8 fresh fillets of sole
> 2 eggs, beaten
> Salt and pepper to taste
> 1 cup fine bread crumbs
> ½ cup + 2 tablespoons imported olive oil
> 2 tablespoons + 1 tablespoon butter
> ⅓ cup dry white wine
> Fresh parsley, chopped, to cook's touch
> Parmesan cheese, grated, to cook's touch
> 1 lemon, sliced, for garnish

Pound the fillets of sole lightly with the flat of a knife blade. Soak them 2 hours in beaten eggs seasoned with salt and pepper. Minutes before serving, roll the fillets in fine bread crumbs and sauté them quickly in ½ cup of olive oil and 2 tablespoons of butter until the coating is light brown. In another skillet, heat the additional 2 tablespoons of olive oil with 1 tablespoon of butter, and again add salt and pepper. Transfer the fish from the first pan to the second, and pour ⅓ cup of dry white wine over the fillets. Cook the fillets until tender, 5 minutes or less. While they are still cooking, sprinkle them with parsley and Parmesan cheese, to the cook's touch. Garnish the sole with slices of lemon and serve piping hot. SERVES 4 AS AN ENTRÉE.

BLANQUIE'S CRAB JACQUES

2 cups large pieces of Dungeness crab meat
½ cup mayonnaise
½ cup chili sauce
¼ cup sweet pickle relish
2 teaspoons Worcestershire sauce
¼ teaspoon tarragon
½ teaspoon minced shallots
Salt and pepper to taste
1 lemon, sliced, for garnish
Fresh parsley, chopped, for garnish

Chill the crab meat. Thoroughly mix together all the other ingredients except the lemon and parsley and chill them. Arrange the crab on a bed of crushed ice. Pour enough of the dressing over the crab to cover it. Serve the rest of the dressing on the side. Garnish the dish with the lemon slices and fresh parsley. SERVES 4 AS AN APPETIZER.

OLD-STYLE SAN FRANCISCO FRENCH ONION SOUP

1 cup sweet butter
4 large white onions
Salt and pepper to taste
3 cups + 3 cups beef stock
¼ cup + ¼ cup milk
4 slices San Francisco or sourdough French bread, toasted
4 tablespoons grated Parmesan cheese or more, to cook's touch, for garnish
4 egg yolks

Melt the butter over low heat in a deep, heavy pan. Cut the onions into large pieces and heat them in the butter, adding salt and pepper, *but do not brown.* Immediately add 3 cups of beef stock along with ¼ cup of milk. Cook 1 hour at a slow simmer, the slower the better. After 1 hour, add the additional 3 cups of beef stock and the additional ¼ cup of milk to the soup mixture, and again simmer slowly for 1 hour. In a separate deep, heavy pan, arrange the 4 slices of the toasted French bread; sprinkle over each a tablespoonful of Parmesan cheese. Just before the soup is finished, beat the 4 egg yolks and add to them 2 tablespoons of the soup. Pour this mixture over the bread and cheese. Cover, and let stand for 5 minutes. Then pour the rest of the soup over the bread and cheese; sprinkle Parmesan cheese on the soup and serve it at once. SERVES 4.

JACQUES' IMPERIAL *Café Brûlot*

4 lumps of sugar
4 whole cloves
3 pieces of lemon peel, twisted
3 pieces of orange peel, twisted
1 piece of vanilla bean
2 sticks of cinnamon
2 jiggers of fine French cognac
5 demitasse cups Jamaica Blue Mountain coffee, black and strong, or espresso may be substituted

In a heated chafing dish, combine the sugar, cloves, lemon peel, orange peel, vanilla bean, cinnamon, and cognac; continue heating until the infusion becomes quite warm. Stir it gently, then carefully touch a match to the cognac until it burns in a sea of leaping blue flames. Let it burn for 30 seconds, then add the coffee. Serve the elegant mixture strained, in demitasse cups. SERVES 6.

DANIEL O'CONNELL, the pure epicure

Photo courtesy of the San Francisco Archives, San Francisco Public Library

Daniel O'Connell

A Street Brawler, a Bohemian Poet, and a Ribald Epicure

"Irish" Dan O'Connell was a dynamic part of San Francisco life for thirty-five years. His biographer, William Greer Harrison, states that "Had he not been a Celt, he would have been a Gypsy!"

Daniel O'Connell was a journalist, athlete, *littérateur*, poet, humorist, dramatist, novelist, and a natural-born chef. He also left an indelible mark of greatness on his beloved city by cofounding the Bohemian Club, that famous bastion of San Francisco's prestigious, powerful men. Harrison describes the dishes O'Connell prepared as "Odes, madrigals, songs, and hymns." It is probably not too far off the mark to say that he drank deeply of more potent libations than those offered by ordinary wells.

Despite all the plays and poetry he wrote, the work O'Connell enjoyed writing the most was *Good Things to Eat and Drink and Where to Get Them*, a thin volume of his hints to the gourmet published in 1918. O'Connell showed no hesitation about praising the things he loved best, including stories of the way John Somali ran the Maison Riche Restaurant, the wonderful times he had with his Bohemian Club pals, and his admiration for Madame Pommery in faraway France. More Pommery wine was sold in San Francisco on a per capita basis than in any city outside France itself. William Wolff, the local importer, organized a booster club for this wonderful vintage, and O'Connell was one of its prime movers.

Possessing tremendous energy, O'Connell was not afraid to take on a fight, with his fists or with his pen. Usually genial and sunny, he was able to function on the various levels of San Francisco life with little trouble. Harrison said, "He dared to question and dared to ask why." Perhaps that is the reason why contemporary newspaper colleagues wrote of him as having been a noble credit to the profession. To his friends, O'Connell was the embodiment of the sensual pleasures of life. He was a leader who attracted a host of followers. He was a vivid person with a type of charisma that other men found irresistible and which was not lost on women, although he was particularly devoted to his wife, Annie Ashley. While the comparison would have made him furious, O'Connell was the predecessor of the late "Enthroned Pro-Consul," Lucius Beebe. Had he lived into the 1920s, O'Connell surely would have been among the designated "Bright People."

Daniel O'Connell did not leave us recipes; he left us a heritage, instead. Some of these ideas are expressed in such poems as "Wine Pictures," which begins:

> *Fill me a brimming goblet,*
> *I said to my winsome wife;*
> *Let me read in its bubbles reflected,*
> *The story of its life.*

And a poem about drunks ends:

> *Must they ever be sinful and erring and weak,*
> *Tottering onward with weary feet,*
> *Stained in the gutter and drunk in the streets?*

O'Connell died at the turn of the century. The elite Bohemian Club honored him as it had honored no other member, with a formal funeral in the Green Room. Before we detail some of O'Connell's legendary and famous recipes, we will honor him with an imaginary feast as a fitting homage to the man and to his incomparable era.

The Menu:

IN THE RED ROOM
A Triumphant Bohemian Feast for "Irish" Dan O'Connell

Antipasto:

San Joaquin Valley Tomatoes, Avocados and Chili con Carne, Asparagus Vinaigrette, and San Francisco Spicy Beets, Conchiglie with Zucchini

Entrées:

Choice of Fricassee of Veal Bohemian, Hawaiian Chicken Kalakaua, or Golden Gate Crab Casserole

Salad:

Mission Dolores Hearts of Palm

Dessert:

Vanilla Soufflé O'Connell with Brandied Cherry Sauce

Appropriate wines and liqueurs

THE BOHEMIAN CLUB, circa 1900

Photo from the authors' private collection

The Recipes:

SAN JOAQUIN VALLEY TOMATOES

3 San Joaquin Valley beefsteak tomatoes
Salt to taste
1 tablespoon lemon juice
Fresh parsley sprigs, for garnish

Chill the tomatoes and slice them. Lightly sprinkle them with the salt and lemon juice, and serve them garnished with fresh parsley sprigs. SERVES 6.

AVOCADOS AND CHILI CON CARNE

1 (28-ounce) can prepared chili con carne
3 ripe California avocados
3 tablespoons lemon juice
1 cup shredded sharp Cheddar cheese
Lettuce leaves, for garnish

Preheat broiler. Heat prepared chili in a saucepan until well heated. Peel and halve the avocados, sprinkle them with lemon juice, and fill the cavities with the well-heated prepared chili con carne. Top each with the sharp Cheddar cheese. Broil just until the cheese melts. Serve the avocado halves, piping hot, on a bed of lettuce leaves. SERVES 6.

ASPARAGUS VINAIGRETTE

½ teaspoon salt
½ teaspoon sugar
1 teaspoon dry mustard
½ teaspoon paprika
½ cup tarragon wine vinegar
6 sprinkles of Tabasco sauce
1 cup imported Italian olive oil
1 clove garlic, crushed
1 pound fresh asparagus, cooked

1 tomato, sliced
1 cup pitted or stuffed green olives
2 fresh mushrooms, sliced
1 hard-boiled egg, quartered, for garnish

Combine the salt, sugar, mustard, and paprika. Add the vinegar, Tabasco, olive oil, and garlic, mixing very well. Pour the dressing into a flat dish; marinate in it for 1 hour the cooked asparagus, tomato, olives, and mushrooms, and then drain them and arrange on a serving plate. Serve the dish chilled, garnished with hard-boiled egg. SERVES 6.

SAN FRANCISCO SPICY BEETS

1 (16-ounce) can sliced red beets, with
  1 cup liquid from the beets
1 cup tarragon vinegar
1 tablespoon sugar
¼ teaspoon allspice
¼ teaspoon cinnamon
6 whole cloves
Lettuce leaves, for garnish

Combine 1 cup of the beet liquid, the tarragon vinegar, sugar, allspice, cinnamon, and cloves in a saucepan. Bring the sauce to a boil and pour it over the drained beets; marinate them for several hours, then drain the beets. Serve the beets chilled, on a bed of lettuce leaves. SERVES 6.

CONCHIGLIE WITH ZUCCHINI

1 cup butter
2 cloves garlic, crushed
4 medium zucchini, sliced
½ cup chopped fresh or frozen chives
1 teaspoon dried rosemary
Salt and pepper to taste
1 pound large pasta shells (conchiglie)
2 tablespoons chopped fresh parsley
½ cup grated Parmesan cheese

Melt the butter in a large skillet. Add the garlic, zu
and cook them until the zucchini slices are cris
rosemary, and season the zucchini to taste with s
move the skillet from the heat. Cook the pasta she
water according to the directions on the package u
but still firm. Drain them *thoroughly*, then add th
quickly return the skillet to the heat and toss th
shells are well coated with butter. Add parsley ar
toss again, and serve the dish at once. SERVES 6.

Lakeside Games, a division of Leisure Dynamics, Inc. Minneapolis, Minnesota 55435

FRICASSEE OF VEAL BOHE

2 pounds leg of veal, cut into 2-in
3 tablespoons arrowroot
½ teaspoon dried basil
Cracked black pepper to taste
½ teaspoon dried oregano, crush
½ teaspoon garlic powder
3 tablespoons bacon fat
3 tablespoons chopped fresh cel
½ cup boiling water, as needed

Dredge the chunks of veal in a mixture of arrowroot and dried seasonings. Brown the dredged meat in the hot bacon fat, and add the
celery leaves. Cover the skillet and cook the meat slowly, in the same
skillet, just until it is tender. Do not overcook it. If the skillet becomes
dry during the cooking, add as much as ½ cup of boiling water.
SERVES 6.

Among other places in the world, O'Connell traveled to the Hawaiian Islands. He became a steadfast champion of the much-maligned
King Kalakaua. Perhaps O'Connell's exotic and noble friend inspired
this recipe:

HAWAIIAN CHICKEN KALAKAUA

3 boneless chicken breasts, skinned and halved
3 tablespoons flour

1 cup + ½ cup butter
½ teaspoon salt
1 tablespoon garlic powder
1 tablespoon arrowroot
2 tablespoons curry powder
1 tablespoon ground black pepper
1 cup milk
½ cup heavy cream
1 egg, beaten

Dredge the chicken breasts in the flour and cook them until tender in 1 cup of the butter. Season them with the salt and set them aside. To make the sauce, first melt the remaining ½ cup of butter in the top of a double boiler, over boiling water. Add the garlic powder and cook the mixture for no more than 1 minute before removing the pan from the boiling water. Now blend in the arrowroot thoroughly, the curry powder, and pepper. In a bowl, combine the milk, heavy cream, and beaten egg, and add these to the butter mixture, once again placing the pan over the boiling water. Stir the sauce constantly until it has thickened. Briefly reheat the chicken breasts, pour the hot sauce over them, and serve them at once. SERVES 6.

GOLDEN GATE CRAB CASSEROLE

¼ cup butter
4 teaspoons flour
1 cup undiluted evaporated milk
¼ cup water
1 tablespoon chopped fresh chives
½ teaspoon dried chervil
1 cup finely sliced celery
2 tablespoons chopped pimento
1½ pounds fresh Dungeness crab meat, cubed
2 hard-boiled eggs, chopped
½ cup slivered, toasted almonds
½ cup buttered bread crumbs
½ cup shredded sharp Cheddar cheese

Preheat oven to 350 degrees F. Melt the butter in a deep pan or skillet. Remove the pan from the heat; stir in the flour, then blend in thoroughly the milk, water, and chives. Return the pan to the heat, and cook the mixture slowly, stirring constantly, until it is thick and smooth. Stir in the chervil, celery, pimento, and crab meat. Add the chopped eggs to the crab mixture, along with the toasted almonds. Pour this into a 1½-quart buttered casserole. Top the casserole with the bread crumbs and cheese, and bake it for 25 minutes, or until it is bubbling hot. SERVES 6.

MISSION DOLORES HEARTS OF PALM

½ cup imported olive oil
2 tablespoons lemon juice
1 teaspoon sugar
½ teaspoon salt
½ teaspoon aromatic bitters
¼ teaspoon paprika
2 tablespoons finely chopped green olives
1 tablespoon dried minced onion
1 tablespoon finely chopped celery
1 (6-ounce) can hearts of palm
1 head of medium limestone lettuce, shredded, to
  cook's touch

Combine the olive oil, lemon juice, sugar, salt, bitters, paprika, olives, onion, celery, and chill them. When ready to serve the salad, toss together the hearts of palm and the limestone lettuce in a large salad bowl. Pour the chilled dressing over the two, toss again, and serve. SERVES 6.

VANILLA SOUFFLÉ O'CONNELL

1 vanilla bean
3 cups milk
2 envelopes unflavored gelatin
1 cup sugar
1 teaspoon salt
4 eggs, separated

½ cup French cognac
1 tablespoon lemon juice
1 teaspoon grated fresh lemon peel
1 teaspoon grated fresh orange peel
½ pint whipping cream
Brandied Cherry Sauce

Split the vanilla bean, scrape out the seeds, and add the pod and seeds to the milk in a saucepan. Combine the gelatin, sugar, and salt, and stir these into the milk. Bring the mixture to a boil, stirring constantly; then remove it from the heat. Beat the egg yolks gently. Beat 1 tablespoon of the hot milk mixture into the egg yolks, then thoroughly blend them into the hot milk mixture. Stir in the cognac, lemon juice, lemon and orange peels. Remove the vanilla bean pod. Chill the mixture until it thickens and mounds on a spoon. Beat the whipping cream until stiff. Beat the egg whites until they are stiff but not dry. Fold the whipped cream into the thickened egg mixture, then fold in the egg whites. Attach a buttered paper or foil collar to a 1½-quart soufflé dish, and pour in the soufflé mixture. Chill it several hours, until set. Remove the collar and serve the soufflé with Brandied Cherry Sauce. SERVES 6.

BRANDIED CHERRY SAUCE

1 (16-ounce) can pitted, dark sweet cherries in syrup
½ teaspoon dried orange peel
1 teaspoon arrowroot
1 tablespoon sugar
1 tablespoon French cognac

Drain the canned cherries, reserving all of the syrup. Combine the cherry syrup with the orange peel, arrowroot, and sugar in a saucepan. Heat the mixture to boiling, stirring constantly, until it just thickens and becomes clear. Then stir in the cognac and cherries. Chill the sauce well. Serve it over portions of the vanilla soufflé.

RAPHAEL WEILL, San Francisco's merry merchant
Photo courtesy of the California Historical Society, San Francisco

Raphael Weill

Merry Merchant and Born Sophisticate

A true *bon vivant* is not likely to be created from whole cloth; the basic threads must be woven within the genes. Raphael Weill, founder of the White House Department Store, was one of those born sophisticates, a breed apart who seem to favor San Francisco at least once a decade. The merry merchant brought French tradition to the City by the Bay in many ways. His store stocked a vast array of imported goods from the European capitals and the latest fashions from Paris. His patronage and personal participation were major factors in the rise of French *haute cuisine* in San Francisco. He was determined that the town would live up to its billing as the "Paris of America."

Pink-cheeked, with a constant twinkle in his eyes, the always elegantly dressed merchant looked the very picture of a sophisticated gourmet. He was unmistakably rich, and he was pleased that his wealth allowed any indulgences. Although he contrived to appear fatherly, the old rogue was a definite danger to the ladies. Weill liked more than just a pretty face, however, and he carefully selected his feminine companions from the leading talents of the musical and theatrical stages. He was seen regularly on-the-town in the most expensive places with such famous stars as Ellen Terry, Nellie Melba, Maxine Elliott, Florence Roberts, Lillian Russell, Julia Marlowe, Vesta Victoria, Emma Calve, and, of course, the exotic, adorable Yvette Guilbert. Glancing backward, it is not for us to judge his motives; rather it is to commend his excellent taste.

Sarah Bernhardt, then at the peak of her acting career, was Raphael Weill's closest actress-friend. When the ravishing Bernhardt played at the Old Orpheum Theater, it was almost impossible to secure a ticket without connections. Weill, however, was pleased to provide seats for his gentlemen friends from the Bohemian Club, where he was a highly visible figure. Weill introduced Bernhardt personally to his Bohemian pals, honoring the vibrant lady with dinners in the Red Room of the exclusive club. The two of them were often seen at Marchand's, Bernhardt's first choice in San Francisco restaurants, perhaps to sample the famous onion soup, a premier dish of this regal room.

Toward the end of his life, Raphael Weill became a San Francisco institution. He was given the Freedom of the City Award. In reality, he could also have had its keys, its treasures, and even the bricks from its streets! The statue of "The Shades," near the balustrade of the California Palace of the Legion of Honor, is dedicated to him. Haig Patigan sculpted a medallion of Weill's features as a tribute from his fellow Bohemians. And the much-decorated San Franciscan received the penultimate honor from his beloved native France: He was invested as a *Chevalier de la Légion d'honneur.* But the accolade that most moved this delightful gentleman was the final homage bestowed on him by his adopted city. On July 11, 1919, Weill returned to San Francisco from France, where he had served during the perils of the Great War. On that day all San Francisco turned out to honor him in a glorious civic reception. He deserved it all.

The following is an authentic but fugitive recipe for the famous dish created in San Francisco in his honor.

CHICKEN RAPHAEL WEILL

3 pounds chicken pieces
4 shallots
½ cup butter
Salt and white pepper to taste
1 jigger of brandy
½ cup chicken stock
½ cup dry white wine
2 teaspoons minced fresh or frozen chives
1 bouquet garni of tarragon and other herbs
Chicken Raphael Weill Sauce
Minced onion for garnish
Fresh parsley sprigs for garnish

Disjoint the chicken pieces; then finely chop the shallots. In a large pan, melt the butter and add the chicken pieces and the shallots. Season them with salt and white pepper, and lightly sauté but do not brown them. Pour the brandy around the edge of the pan, light it carefully, and let the flame die away. Then add the chicken stock, white wine, chives, and the bouquet garni. Cover the pan, and cook the chicken until it is tender. Remove the bouquet garni and the chicken pieces. Save juices in the pan. Serve the chicken with this special sauce. SERVES 6.

CHICKEN RAPHAEL WEILL SAUCE

1½ cups heavy cream
Pan juices from chicken
2 tablespoons dry sherry
Salt and white pepper to taste
3 egg yolks, lightly beaten

Add the heavy cream to the juices remaining in the pan, then add the sherry, salt, and white pepper, and heat but do not boil the mixture. Then gradually add the yolks to the sauce, stirring constantly until it thickens. Pour it over the chicken, and garnish the dish with minced onion and parsley sprigs.

COLONEL JOHN C. KIRKPATRICK, manager of the Palace Hotel
Photo courtesy of the California Historical Society, San Francisco

Colonel John C. Kirkpatrick
The Thirty-Thousand-Dollar Hotelier

The absentee owners of the Palace Hotel paid Colonel John C. Kirkpatrick thirty thousand dollars a year to manage the deluxe Market Street hostelry. In those days, this salary was considered stupendous. Kirkpatrick's lucrative wages shocked the hotel community—until it became apparent that the wise directors had made a sterling investment. Kirkpatrick earned annually twenty-four thousand dollars *more* than was paid the governor of California. And, when the Palace's board consented to pay him that vast sum, it also agreed to a hands-off policy, allowing the experienced hotelier total freedom in running "the house." Yet . . . the colonel was not a master chef nor a promotional wizard nor a meticulous housekeeper. He applied his special genius to the total functioning of the hotel, and thereby it became the finest of its kind in the West.

Ernest Arbogast, for more than twenty years *chef de cuisine* at the Palace Hotel, worked with Kirkpatrick harmoniously. The chef understood what the colonel wanted in the way of culinary triumphs, and he provided them with regularity. Arbogast created two memorable dishes in the colonel's name. Oysters Kirkpatrick has become a classic preparation: Arbogast sprinkled crisp bacon over oysters on the half-shell, added butter and catsup, and topped off the bivalves with freshly grated Parmesan cheese. The inventive chef then placed the oysters in an oven for 10 minutes' baking and served them piping hot. Eggs Kirkpatrick must have been equally delicious. Unfortunately, Arbogast's exact recipe for the casserole has not survived, but we know it was a tomato-and-egg mixture, probably concocted to help the high-living, portly hotel manager recover from one of his frequent hangovers.

Kirkpatrick and Arbogast were an unbeatable pair of collaborators. With Arbogast's help, the colonel left an indelible benchmark in dining to his beloved adopted city. It was a standard that has rarely been matched in San Francisco or any other city.

Joseph Tilden
A Gentleman in the Kitchen

In his time, Major Joseph Tilden was the most notable culinary member of the Bohemian Club. He was the presiding genius at many of the club's banquets as well as a leader of summertime "High-Jinks"— parodies within the confines of the Bohemian Grove in Sonoma County. A cook and a clubman, Tilden was also something of an adventurer. His unexpected, hurried departure for Hawaii in 1884— a considerable undertaking in those days—was heralded at the club by a farewell banquet, which must have been both delicious and rowdy. Daniel O'Connell, who was later to follow Tilden to Hawaii, was one of the principal speakers. Tilden left no record of his personal adventures in the Pacific except that he dubbed Honolulu "wild and dangerous"—although, like his friend, O'Connell, he also strongly defended the eccentric King Kalakaua. After Tilden's death in the early 1900s, some of his friends at the club, in a typical Bohemian gesture, paid for the publication of a charming little book of *Joe Tilden's Recipes for Epicureans*. The book is a fitting tribute to his unusual culinary talents. Some sample recipes:

TOASTED ANGELS

8 large oysters
Cayenne pepper to taste
4 drops of lime juice
8 thinly sliced strips of bacon

Preheat broiler. Remove the oysters from their shells. Sprinkle the cayenne pepper and lime juice over oysters. Wrap each oyster in a thin strip of bacon and fasten it with a wooden toothpick. Place them on a rack with drip pan. Broil the oysters until the bacon is crisp, and serve them very hot. SERVES 2 AS AN APPETIZER.

BACALOS AL VISCAINA

½ medium salted codfish
1 large green pepper, sliced
2 tablespoons + ¼ cup olive oil
2 onions, chopped
2 large tomatoes, chopped
Salt and pepper to taste

Soak salted codfish overnight in water. Drain, thoroughly rinse, and then dry the fish. Sauté the sliced green pepper in 2 tablespoons of olive oil, and then set the slices aside and drain. In a large saucepan, heat the additional ¼ cup of olive oil and brown the onions. Then add the tomatoes and, over low heat, stew the mixture for 15 minutes. Bone the fish, cut it into small pieces, and add it to the mixture. Cook this over low heat for ½ hour more, seasoning to taste with salt and pepper. Serve on a platter topped with sautéed green peppers. SERVES 6 AS AN ENTRÉE.

DEVILED PORK CHOPS

4 large rib pork chops
1 ounce butter
1 teaspoon dry mustard
½ teaspoon prepared mustard
1 teaspoon freshly grated horseradish or prepared horseradish
1 teaspoon chutney
4 drops of vinegar
Juice of 1 lime
Salt and pepper to taste
Dash of cayenne pepper to taste
Tabasco sauce to taste

Preheat broiler. Coat the pork chops with ⅔ of the dressing made of the rest of the ingredients and broil until well done. Pour the remaining ⅓ of the sauce over the chops and serve them in a very hot dish. SERVES 4 AS AN ENTRÉE.

EGGS WITH TOMATOES

2 medium white onions, chopped
2 medium green peppers, chopped
2 ounces butter
6 fresh tomatoes, peeled and sliced
Salt and pepper to taste
½ cup cooked corn kernels
6 eggs

Preheat oven to 350 degrees F. In a skillet, sauté the onions and green peppers in the butter. Add the tomatoes and salt and pepper to taste and simmer the mixture for 15 minutes. Add the corn kernels and cook it another 15 minutes. Pour the mixture into a large greased baking dish. Break 6 eggs into the surface and bake until eggs are set. SERVES 6 AS AN ENTRÉE.

TILDEN'S FIVE FAMOUS CHAMPAGNE CUPS

As for the suggested servings for all five bubbly recipes listed below, we believe that the choices are best left to the impeccable discretion of the particular hosts and hostesses—and their guests!

TILDEN CUP NUMBER ONE

1 cucumber, peeled and sliced
1 pint sherry
½ pint brandy
Rind of 2 lemons, grated
Juice of 1 lemon
Juice of 3 oranges
½ pint curaçao
3 bottles of champagne
2 quart bottles of seltzer water or any carbonated water
3 quart bottles of apollinaris or any mineral water or
   light ginger ale
Sugar to taste
Ice

Pour over the sliced cucumber in a large punch bowl, the sherry and brandy. Add the grated lemon rind. Pour in the lemon and orange juices, curaçao, champagne, seltzer water or any carbonated water, and substitute mineral water or light ginger ale for the apollinaris. Finally, sweeten the cup to taste and ice it well. The long-vanished apollinaris water may have come from a now-extinct mineral spring near the Palace of Fine Arts, possibly owned by Apolonario Miranda.

TILDEN CUP NUMBER TWO

2 tablespoons sugar
Juice and finely grated peel of 1 lemon
1 cucumber, peeled and sliced
1 wineglass of curaçao
1 quart apollinaris or any mineral water or light ginger ale
1 quart champagne
1 block of ice

Mix together the sugar, lemon juice and peel, cucumber, curaçao, mineral water or light ginger ale for the apollinaris, and champagne. Pour the mixture over the block of ice in a large punch bowl.

TILDEN CUP NUMBER THREE

3 ounces sugar
Juice of 4 lemons
Rind of 1 lemon
1 quart apollinaris or any mineral water or light ginger ale
1 quart orgeat
1 pint brandy
½ wineglass of Jamaican rum
1 wineglass of maraschino
3 quarts of champagne
Ice

Combine the sugar, lemon juice and rind, mineral water or light ginger ale for the apollinaris, then the orgeat. Stir the mixture well. Then add brandy, rum, and maraschino. Strain the ingredients into a large bowl with plenty of ice. Just before serving, pour the champagne.

TILDEN CUP NUMBER FOUR

2 tablespoons sugar
Peel of 1 lemon
Juice of ½ lemon
3 slices fresh pineapple
1 wineglass of maraschino
1 wineglass of brandy
1 quart apollinaris or any mineral water or light ginger ale
1 quart champagne
Ice

Mix together the sugar, lemon peel and juice, the slices of pineapple, maraschino, and brandy. Substitute mineral water or light ginger ale for the apollinaris. Add the champagne. Ice well and serve.

TILDEN CUP NUMBER FIVE

2 ounces sugar
Peel and juice of 1 orange
2 wineglasses of sherry
1 wineglass of maraschino
1 quart apollinaris or any mineral water or light ginger ale
1 quart champagne
1 cucumber, peeled and sliced
Ice

Mix the sugar with the orange peel. Add the orange juice, sherry, maraschino, and mineral water or light ginger ale for the apollinaris. Then add the champagne, the slices of cucumber, and plenty of ice.

Victor Hirtzler

The Triumphs of an Imperial Chef

If Victor Hirtzler, the world-famous *chef de cuisine* at the St. Francis Hotel from 1906 to 1925, had been told that he was responsible in part for the ghastly assassination of a king, he would surely have denied it with an explosion of French expletives. Yet Hirtzler did seduce the King of Portugal, Dom Carlos, into hosting banquets so extravagant and posh that the kingdom's treasury went bankrupt. Dom Carlos' huge expenditures were among the failures that provoked the murder of the unfortunate monarch.

History should excuse Hirtzler's titled patron for his folly. It would have been almost impossible for Dom Carlos, or anybody else for that matter, to refuse the preparation of an entrée such as Mousse Faison Lucullus, the Bavarian pheasant breast stuffed with truffles and woodcock and served with a champagne, cognac, and Madeira sauce. The lavish dish cost $180 a serving! It was first concocted in 1900 for a hundred court guests, and it quickly became the exotic centerpiece for an orgy of gastronomic indulgences.

Another tale that surrounds the volatile Strasbourger is that, at one time, he was the official food taster for the Czar of All the Russias, Nicholas II. Fortunately, nobody attempted to poison the czar while Hirtzler was employed at the Imperial Court. At one point, however, the high-strung chef's ministrations seem to have caused the downfall of a politico who *almost* became head of state. In 1916, Hirtzler prepared a lavish luncheon in San Francisco's respected Commercial Club in honor of Charles Evans Hughes, candidate for the presidency of the United States and a clear front-runner. Ten minutes before the food was to be served, the waiters walked out on strike. Undaunted, Hirtzler proceeded to serve Hughes himself, and he also pressed the kitchen staff into serving the other guests. This so outraged the striking culinary workers that they circulated flyers throughout the state charging Hughes with antiunion bias. On election eve, the popular candidate was confident. But the next morning he awoke to find he had lost

VICTOR HIRTZLER, the incomparable chef of the St. Francis Hotel
Photo courtesy of the St. Francis Hotel

California by fewer than four thousand votes—enough to cost him the election.

Victor Hirtzler's menus and recipes are preserved in the *Hotel St. Francis Book of Recipes and Menus*, first published in 1910 and reprinted several times thereafter. The recipes substantiate Hirtzler's description of his life's profession as *l'art culinaire*.

Victor Hirtzler is the only turn-of-the-century *chef de cuisine* to be immortalized in our time by the naming of a restaurant. Victor's, the award-winning establishment atop the thirty-second floor of the Hotel St. Francis, perpetuates his culinary fame, as does this simple dish:

VICTOR HIRTZLER'S SOLE EDWARD VII

8 fillets of sole
Salt and ground pepper to taste
1 cup sweet butter
3 ounces chopped salted almonds
1 cup chopped fresh mushrooms
2 tablespoons minced fresh parsley
Juice of 1 lemon
Nutmeg, to cook's touch
½ cup dry white wine

Preheat oven to 350 degrees F. Lay the fillets on a board and lightly pound them with the flat of a knife. Arrange a single layer of the fillets in a buttered pan, season them with salt and ground pepper, and spread over them a mixture of the butter, almonds, mushrooms, parsley, lemon juice, and nutmeg. Add the wine to the pan, and bake the fillets for 20 to 25 minutes. Chef Victor liked to serve the sole directly from the pan, carrying it on a platter, the whole covered by a white napkin. SERVES 4 AS AN ENTRÉE.

II.

THE LUCULLAN HOTELS

As the new century began, San Francisco was considered among those American cities with an acceptable choice of deluxe hotels able to please even the most fastidious crowned heads of Europe. In San Francisco, the tradition started early, only a decade or so after the Gold Rush. The Occidental Hotel, the Lick House, and the Baldwin Hotel were among the leading hostelries of the nation in the nineteenth century. The Baldwin, on the corner of Market and Powell, sat on what is now the site of the Flood Building. However, the fabulous Palace Hotel, inaugurated in October of 1875, immediately surpassed all the previous efforts of its competitors. Overnight, the new house gained a reputation as the best hotel in the West. Nothing could match the style and splendor of the Palace until the St. Francis opened in 1904, followed by the Fairmont in 1907.

The older establishments were not to be entirely discounted when it came to the sensual pleasures, however. For instance, the Earlcourt, a chic, small hotel, satisfyingly catered to such luminaries as Adelina Patti, Nellie Melba, and Sarah Bernhardt. As early as April 1868, Anson Burlingame entertained 225 local dignitaries at a marvelous banquet at the Lick House that honored a group of ambassadors from the Manchu Court. Even if the Chinese noblemen did not recognize all the elaborate dishes on the menu, we may presume they were impressed with the decorations. Six gigantic pyramids dominated the main dining room. Startling, beautiful, and terribly expensive, these obelisks represented a Chinese pagoda, a double horn of plenty, the steamer *Colorado* on which the Sino delegation had arrived in San Francisco Bay, a majestic Corbeille of Nougat, one of the magical, shimmering waterfalls from the Palace of Versailles, and a Croquembouche garnished with prized California fruit that staggered the imagination!

Could anybody seriously doubt that these illustrious gentlemen from the Celestial Kingdom were thoroughly impressed by their opulent reception in San Francisco . . . ?

LICK HOUSE HOTEL, the main dining room
Photo courtesy of the California Historical Society, San Francisco

THE EARLCOURT HOTEL, a favorite of luminous ladies
Photo courtesy of the San Francisco Archives, San Francisco Public Library

The Palace

Shortly after the doors opened, a glittering civic banquet was given at the Palace on October 14, 1875, in honor of General Philip H. Sheridan. The menu for this glamorous event was prepared by Jules Harder, the first of a long line of magnificent chefs to grace the kitchens of this gracious hotel, all of whom contributed to San Francisco's knowledge and admiration of *haute cuisine*. By the time Ernest Arbogast was in charge as *premier chef*, the city was eager to accept almost any new epicurean experience. Arbogast, nobody's fool, was quick to take advantage of his patrons' adventurous spirit, and he created a series of memorable dishes, some of which he named for the celebrities of the day. When the honored chef retired after more than twenty years of service, the tradition of culinary perfection was maintained at the Palace by his successor, Jules Dauvillier.

The Palace reigned supreme in San Francisco as "the place to stay and be seen" until the terrifying early morning hours of April 18, 1906. At 5:13 A.M., one hundred miles up the rugged Northern California coast from the hotel's Market Street location, a violent shock sprang from the sea and rushed ashore near desolate Point Arena. It traveled quickly down the spine of the bordering hills, shot beneath the Golden Gate, and leaped along the mountains of the South Bay Peninsula, devastating everything in its path. As a final act of brutal destruction before petering out in the Salinas Valley, the earthquake leveled completely the charming old Mission San Juan Bautista. "The temblor gave our joyous and breezy town a jolt that will live in history," David Starr Jordan, then president of Stanford University, was to correctly prophesy later.

The powerful initial shock wave caused only a superficial amount of damage to the Palace—the massive caravansary had been designed to withstand *almost* anything—resulting in some cracked plaster, instances of buckling throughout the marble flooring, and broken glass.

THE OLD PALACE HOTEL, as it looked before the earthquake
of 1906
Photo courtesy of the San Francisco Archives, San Francisco Public Library

For the moment, at least, the structure stood almost unscathed. However, the glorious old hotel soon faced a new danger. Shortly after nine o'clock that morning, a cluster of small fires that began south of Market adjacent to the Palace quickly merged to become a single giant conflagration. The city's water supply had already failed, but the hotel staff consoled themselves with knowledge of the 675,000-gallon water reservoir beneath the Garden Court.

The self-assigned hotel brigade fought the blaze valiantly, but was no match for the raging firestorm. Finally, at two-thirty in the afternoon, the Palace's great reservoir had run dry, and the gallant band was forced to abandon the fight. By four o'clock, the "Old Palace" was no more. A "New Palace" eventually rose on the old site, but no mere reproduction, no matter how noble, could equal the splendor of the original hotel's reputation or the triumph of its halcyon years.

Chef Jules Dauvillier, who had been paid the astounding sum of ten thousand dollars to cook for Mr. and Mrs. Harry Payne Whitney when he first arrived in New York, created these dishes for the Palace Hotel:

TEN-THOUSAND-DOLLAR CALF'S LIVER AND BACON
À LA DAUVILLIER

> 8 slices of bacon
> 1 large fresh calf's liver
> Salt and pepper to taste
> ⅓ cup olive oil
> Bercy Butter

Preheat broiler. Broil the slices of bacon. Drain. Trim the calf's liver of membranes and slice it into 8 pieces. Season them with salt and pepper, then sauté in the very hot oil over a quick fire until brown. Arrange them on a heated platter with the bacon slices and the chef's secret: Spread the liver with Bercy butter. SERVES 4 AS AN ENTRÉE.

BERCY BUTTER

> ½ cup sweet butter
> Shallots, chopped, to cook's touch

Fresh parsley, chopped, to cook's touch
Fresh chervil, chopped, to cook's touch
1 tablespoon dry white wine
Freshly ground black pepper to taste

Mix the sweet butter with some chopped shallots, parsley, and chervil. Add the spoonful of wine, and grind in the black pepper to taste. Blend the ingredients well.

During the lush years between 1875 and 1906, the most popular breakfasts served in the Ladies Grill at the Palace Hotel featured the oyster. Here is Chef Ernest Arbogast's way of preparing oysters and eggs:

CALIFORNIA OYSTER OMELET *À LA ARBOGAST*

1 dozen small oysters
6 eggs
1 small onion, finely chopped
1 tablespoon flour
1 tablespoon butter
½ cup heavy cream
Salt and pepper to taste
Fresh parsley sprigs, for garnish
Paprika, for garnish

Remove oysters from their shells. Beat eggs thoroughly, add the chopped onion, and cook the mixture slowly over low heat in a buttered omelet pan. In another pan over medium heat, mix the flour and butter into a paste, then add the heavy cream. Simmer the sauce until it begins to thicken; then bring the sauce to the boiling point, and remove it from the fire. Drain the oysters and then stir them into the sauce. Add salt and pepper to taste. When the egg and onion mixtures are as firm as desired, pour the creamed oysters over the eggs and fold over the omelets. Serve them on hot plates with fresh parsley sprigs and colorful sprinkles of paprika. SERVES 2.

The Fairmont

Mr. and Mrs. Herman Oelrichs were secure in the pantheon of exclusive Nob Hill society at the century's turn. She was the former Tessie Fair, daughter of the senator, James Fair. About her, James Pelton wrote rapturously:

> *That love-lit face; that modest mien;*
> *That warmly throbbing heart;*
> *That spotless life, in truth agleam,*
> *Defies the powers of art.*

Herman Oelrichs was a successful businessman and *bon vivant* friend of Raphael Weill. After the death of her husband, Tessie Fair Oelrichs set about building a hotel atop Nob Hill that would resemble a palace and become the height of fashion and elegance. The classical architect Stanford White was hired to design the building. Mrs. Oelrichs thought White's ambitious plan was the triumph she needed to crown her beloved "Hill." The widow spared no expense on the project and even lent a series of priceless mirrors from her collection to decorate the splendid lobby. After delays occasioned by the dark events of April 1906, the Fairmont opened in 1907.

By 1908, there was unanimous agreement about town that San Francisco's three great hotels were first-class in every way. But society accorded each a leading edge in different categories. At the Palace, it was the food. At the St. Francis (having been built in 1904), it was the location. But the new Fairmont led in entertainment. Nor has the hotel been surpassed in this department during the many years of its existence. Time and an immense amount of money have been spent to make its unique public rooms an entertainment in themselves. San Francisco was captivated with dining at a superior hotel without having to leave its confines to be entertained later in the evening. Successive managements, and now the Swig family, have preserved the Fairmont's original flair for showmanship.

THE FAIRMONT HOTEL in the early 1900s, as designed by
Stanford White
Photo courtesy of the San Francisco Archives, San Francisco Public Library

Since the Fairmont's early success, it has become the first San Francisco deluxe hostelry to spawn others under the same name and management in other United States cities. Members of the Swig family have proved themselves to be superb innkeepers in the finest sense of the word.

This is the particularly luxurious version of Sauce Mornay that was served at the Fairmont Hotel in the early halcyon days:

MORNAY—THE COSTLIEST SAUCE

2 tablespoons + 2 tablespoons butter
2 tablespoons flour
1 cup milk
Salt to taste
1 tablespoon freshly grated Parmesan cheese
1 tablespoon flaked Gruyère cheese

In a saucepan over very low heat, melt 2 tablespoons of the butter until it is clarified but not browned. Stir in the flour, blending well. In another saucepan, bring the 1 cup of milk almost to a boil, and, while still stirring the butter-and-flour mixture, add the hot milk all at once. This mixture will thicken when it comes to a slight boil; then simmer it gently and carefully for about 5 minutes. Stir and watch. Do not take your eyes off the sauce. Season it with salt to taste.

Using a wire whisk, beat into the hot mixture the grated Parmesan cheese and flaked Gruyère cheese. Keep the sauce over a low heat, stirring constantly, until the cheeses melt, but do not let it come to a boil. Finally, blend in the remaining 2 tablespoons of butter, a little at a time. *Voilà!* Sauce Mornay!

TOP O' THE HILL SQUAB CHICKEN

Chef Emile Burgermeister's Squab Chicken as he prepared it at the Fairmont:

Salt and pepper to taste
4 small squab chickens
8 small new peeled potatoes
1 cup pure vegetable oil

THE ANNUAL SOCIETY FLOWER SHOW at the Fairmont Hotel
Photo courtesy of the San Francisco Archives, San Francisco Public Library

Button mushrooms, to cook's touch
4 tablespoons butter
1 medium onion, sliced
1 large carrot, chopped
Fresh artichoke hearts, to cook's touch
Truffles, to cook's touch

Preheat oven to 350 degrees F. Salt and pepper the squab chickens
and let them stand for 2 hours in the refrigerator. Meanwhile, prepare
the vegetables: With a small scoop, cut out pieces of the potatoes
the size of a large olive and deep-fry them in hot oil for 1 minute.
Remove them from the oil and set aside to drain. Wash and drain
the button mushrooms. Clarify the butter and pour it in a thin film
over the squab chickens. Place the chickens side by side in a large
roasting pan. Roast the chickens in the oven until just golden brown;
then add the onion slices, the carrot, the deep-fried potatoes, the artichoke hearts, mushrooms, and truffles. Cover the roasting pan tightly
and cook the birds and vegetables for another hour. Trim each bird
with the vegetables when ready for serving. SERVES 4 AS AN ENTRÉE.

THE ST. FRANCIS HOTEL as it was in the early part of this
century
Photo courtesy of the San Francisco Archives, San Francisco Public Library

The St. Francis

How many San Franciscans can still remember the old saying "Meet me at the 'Frantic' under the clock?" The affectionate nickname was bestowed upon the St. Francis Hotel almost from the day it opened in 1904. And, as far as the natives were concerned, there might have been only one "clock" in all downtown San Francisco!

The free-standing rococo timepiece in the main lobby was a masterpiece of European craftsmanship. After its installation in the old-world reception area, the clock added immensely to the luxurious impression of the hostelry. When the sharp-tongued novelist Gertrude Atherton agreed to pose for a figure representing "California" in a mural by Albert Herter to be prominently displayed in the Mural Room, she could not have known that she would be upstaged by a *clock*. Mrs. Atherton, in the heat of an altercation with her frequent British antagonist George Moore called him "A codfish crossed with a satyr!" What would she have been tempted to call an upstaging clock?

Situated with its face toward Union Square and the towering column of the Admiral Dewey Monument, the St. Francis has become an indelible part of the city's central lifestyle. From the very start, the hotel's managers seized the opportunity to capture a thriving luncheon business. The various public restaurants, artfully placed throughout the first floor, were pleasantly inviting and convenient. The private dining rooms on the second floor proved to be ideal for corporate and club occasions. No single explanation will tell us why the St. Francis became the premier hotel for socialites to favor for lunch. The trend may have started because of the richness of its furniture and the opulence of the table settings; or perhaps because the town's wealthiest and most beautiful women are viewed to their supreme advantage at the hotel in rooms deliberately arranged for this purpose. Whichever, lunch at the St. Francis is still a "must" whether one is a visitor or a native.

Many dishes, classics in their day, have come and gone in our city, but Celery Victor continues, seemingly forever. It was invented by Chef Victor Hirtzler for the St. Francis. Several shortcuts, all quite honorable, make it easy to prepare. It takes well to personal touches by the inventive cook. The chef himself had one sterling piece of advice: "Use very sharp white vinegar!"

ST. FRANCIS CELERY VICTOR

6 stalks of celery
1 cup chicken or veal stock
Salt and pepper to taste
2 bay leaves
Other herbs and spices, as desired
¼ cup sharp white vinegar, flavored with tarragon
¾ cup imported olive oil
Ground chervil, to cook's touch
Garnishes, as desired

Marinate the celery, well washed, for 1 hour in a stock of the cook's own choice. Canned broth is a perfectly acceptable substitute for homemade stock from chicken or veal bones. To this basic stock add salt, if needed, ground pepper to taste, bay leaves, and other herbs and spices as desired. After marinating the celery, boil it gently in the same stock until it is almost soft; then remove the celery from the broth and allow it to drain and cool. Carefully press out the remaining liquid by hand. Arrange the celery on a serving platter and chill it in the refrigerator. Mix a dressing of the tarragon vinegar, olive oil, ground chervil, and salt and pepper to taste. Pour the dressing over the chilled celery. Garnish the platter with fresh parsley sprigs, sliced hard-boiled eggs, cold cooked asparagus spears, or other cold accompaniments. Anchovies may be laid across the celery, just before serving, for added interest. SERVES 6 AS A SIDE DISH.

Most of the famous dishes served to the guests at the St. Francis Hotel during its early years were recorded in Victor Hirtzler's cookbook. Here are two of his favorite sauces:

CREAM HORSERADISH SAUCE

2 tablespoons butter
1 heaping tablespoon flour
1 cup heavy cream
1 cup milk
Salt and pepper to taste
1 teaspoon powdered sugar
1 small bottle of prepared horseradish

Melt the butter in a pan, add the flour, and then mix them thoroughly. Add the heavy cream and milk, again mixing thoroughly, and cook the sauce over low heat until it thickens. Season it with salt and pepper to taste. It should now be of an even, creamy consistency. If the sauce is too thick, add milk. Finally, mix in the powdered sugar and prepared horseradish. Serve hot.

ROMAN SAUCE

1 cup finely chopped celery root
1 tablespoon coriander seeds
1 tablespoon powdered sugar
1 clove garlic, crushed
1 handful of fresh parsley, chopped
1 bay leaf
2 cups white wine
1 cup brown sauce
Juice of 1 lemon
1 cup sultana raisins
1 tablespoon butter
1 wineglass of Madeira

In a stainless steel or enamel-lined pan, simmer the celery root in a little water until it is tender. Add to the pan the coriander seeds, powdered sugar, the garlic clove, the parsley, bay leaf, and white wine. Simmer them together for 20 minutes. If more liquid must be added, use wine. Then add the brown sauce and the lemon juice. Stir the sauce and strain it. Add the sultana raisins, butter, and Madeira. Serve hot. Both of the above sauces may be served with game and other highly flavored meats and fowl. EACH RECIPE SERVES 4 MEAT DISHES.

THE MAGNIFICENT OLD LOBBY OF THE ST. FRANCIS
HOTEL
Photo courtesy of the San Francisco Archives, San Francisco Public Library

THE ST. FRANCIS HOTEL CLOCK, the clock at the "Frantic"
Photo courtesy of the San Francisco Archives, San Francisco Public Library

III.
"IT WAS INVENTED IN SAN FRANCISCO!"

SAN FRANCISCO AND THE OPULENT OYSTER HAVE THIS THING IN COMMON: You can't talk about either one of them and not think about sex! Julius Caesar and his brawny cohorts discovered the oyster in Britain, and the effects of those sweet morsels could well have led to the eventual decline of the Empire. During the Golden Decades, life in San Francisco was a continuing Saturnalia, so it is not surprising that the Bay City version of the oyster cocktail was first served at Gobey's Restaurant on Sutter Street in the late 1800s. Another favorite San Franciscan oyster item was "The Squarer"; it was eaten just like the famous hamburger of today. The Squarer began with a loaf of white bread with its top portion cut off and its insides hollowed out. The loaf was then smeared with butter, toasted, and finally filled with oysters that had been lightly fried in more butter. The fast-food clerks of that time merely put the top part of the bread back on, wrapped the loaf, and sent it gaily off with the usually hung-over customer munching happily away.

Bacchanalian San Francisco demolished willpower and thus greatly encouraged excruciating "day-after" effects, whether from an excess of aphrodisiacal activity, heavy drinking, overeating, or a common combination of all three temptations. In those naughty days, long-suffering wives were hardly surprised when their philandering husbands dropped dead at an early age from anemia, kidney failure, or rotten livers. Contributing heavily to the general demise of the natives were such strong whiskey-based drinks as "The Bonanza"; "The Black Velvet," which was velvet champagne with a float of stout; and "The Stone Wall," concocted with rum and cider. Over the years, writers have repeated the myth that the Sazerac cocktail was an invention of the Gold Rush bars. A liking for the Sazerac demanded an acquired taste and a zinc-lined stomach. This drink was made from rye, absinthe, and bitters shaken with ice and served in a glass rubbed with anisette. San Franciscans drank gallons of this devil's brew, but there

57

is little doubt that the Sazerac first sprang from the sinful roots of New Orleans.

Professor Jerry Thomas, the most famous local bartender of his day, invented the Blue Blazer and proudly served it in the tent that, in 1850, was the El Dorado Saloon. He published its secret in a small booklet, *How to Mix Drinks:*

PROFESSOR JERRY THOMAS' AMAZING BLUE BLAZER

> 1 ample wineglass of scotch whiskey
> Boiling water
> Peel of 1 lemon
> 2 teaspoons sugar

Pour in each of 2 silver mugs an ample wineglass of scotch whiskey. Add to the whiskey enough boiling water that the scotch becomes warm enough to ignite. Prepare with caution! Set both mugs afire, and mix their contents by pouring the flaming liquid from mug to mug 4 or 5 times in a continuous stream of fire. The professor notes that this technique may take practice; he suggests first trying it cold. Serve each drink in a bar tumbler with half the lemon peel and a teaspoon of sugar. SERVES 2.

The Blue Blazer is dramatic, but another invention of the professor's is immortal:

THE CLASSIC TOM AND JERRY

> 2 large eggs
> ¼ cup sugar
> 2 ounces dark rum
> ½ teaspoon ground cinnamon
> ¼ teaspoon ground cloves
> 1 pint hot bourbon or rye
> 1 quart hot milk or half-and-half

Beat the whole eggs and, just as they are beginning to get thick, gradually add the sugar. Continue beating the mixture until it is very stiff. Add the rum, cinnamon, and cloves, and beat the batter again. Spoon it into 8 small mugs. Add 2 ounces of hot but not boiled bourbon or rye to each mug, and then fill the mug with hot milk or half-and-half. Stir the drinks and serve them while they are still very hot. SERVES 8.

Certainly, Professor Thomas did not invent the Mint Julep, but more of it was consumed in a week on the downtown Cocktail Route than in a month anywhere else in the country. San Franciscans had their own exclusive version of the drink:

THE GREAT SAN FRANCISCO MINT JULEP

Dash of fresh mint, crumpled
Dash of powdered sugar
1 jigger of bourbon whiskey
Dash of Jamaican rum
Fresh mint sprigs for garnish
Additional powdered sugar for garnish

Bruise several sprigs of fresh mint with a little powdered sugar in a mixing glass. Fill the glass with ice and pour the jigger of bourbon over it. Let this stand for 10 minutes, then add a dash of Jamaican rum. Serve the julep with long straws in a fresh chilled glass, dressed with more sprigs of mint and a sprinkling of powdered sugar. SERVES 1.

San Francisco has always adored grand opera. Singers of international repute who graced the city's many stages and then announced that they "loved" the town were likely to be embraced by the populace forever. The Spanish *prima donna assoluta* Adelina Patti (her real name was Adela Juana Maria Patti) received a most fervent tribute. For her, Chef Ernest Arbogast created "Patti Consommé" at the Palace Hotel. The dish was made with small chicken dumplings, hearts of artichokes, and spaghetti, all simmered in chicken broth.

It is not generally known that the modest but delicious Mexican *enchilada* was first introduced to *gringos* at San Francisco's Ingleside Race Track in the 1890s. Another "first" was the popularization of "Hangtown Fry" as the recipe traveled from Placerville in the Sierra foothills to the Old Fly Trap Restaurant at 73 Sutter Street in the heart of San Francisco's business district.

In the next century, the Palace Hotel chef created Green Goddess Dressing in honor of George Arliss, the renowned actor who was starring in *The Green Goddess* in San Francisco at the time. The actor frequently complimented San Francisco's marvelous weather which, he swore, induced a healthy appetite.

Brillat-Savarin was completely convinced only a genius could make a great sauce. Louis Coutard was neither genius nor a professional *saucier;* yet he was inspired to originate San Francisco's own "Louis Dressing." This particular sauce has spoiled generations of natives who cannot bear to eat anything else with cold shrimp, prawns, crab, or lobster. Natives even were known to prefer "Louis Dressing" on— horrors!—bowls of plain naked lettuce. For them, as for so many since then, "Thousand Island" was a distinctly disappointing substitute for the one-and-only:

THE ORIGINAL LOUIS DRESSING

1 part olive oil
1 part chili sauce
Fresh chives, chopped, to cook's touch
Fresh parsley, chopped, to cook's touch
1 part red wine vinegar
Salt and pepper to taste
Dash powdered mustard
Lemon juice to taste

Thoroughly stir together all the ingredients and serve the dressing quite chilled. It becomes tastier after it has aged for several days in the refrigerator. When dining in San Francisco, please be sure to ask for *Loo-e-e-e* Dressing, as dyed-in-the-wool San Francisco waiters simply will not recognize the sauce by any other name!

It's very surprising that few original dishes were created and named for the many great actresses who graced our thriving, packed theaters of every kind. Even the divine Sarah Bernhardt, who favored Marchand's with her patronage when in town, failed to snare that coveted honor. Typically, San Francisco did honor a risqué revue called *The Black Crook* that was banned nearly everywhere but was allowed to play here. It featured adorable ladies in skin-hugging tights and precious little else. Night after night in San Francisco, soused gents trampled each other for front-row seats, and the ladies of the chorus could be assured of sold-out houses. This notorious theatrical event was commemorated by the invention of a drink whose recipe is lost to us. We can only speculate that the palate was as delighted by the libation as is the imagination titillated by its name: "Tight Henry's Tights"! The culinary firsts that followed, if not as smile-provoking as "The Tights," are nonetheless quite as characteristic of San Francisco.

Oh Yes! There Was a Free Lunch!

It may come as no surprise at all that San Francisco popularized the cocktail, establishing in the 1880s a near-sacred, never-varying "Cocktail Route" that was pursued at a leisurely pace, from bar to bar, by such notables as Senator William Sharon and his compatriots. Hand-in-glove with the Cocktail Route was another San Francisco invention called the Free Lunch. Gentlemen (and surely others!) could partake of the free food or pay for the commercial lunch of the day, if preferred. The Free Lunch tables always had an immense assortment of foods, everything from salamis to salmon, imported and domestic items, and appropriate garnishes for a buffet serving. There seemed to be no end to the succulent tidbits. Any honest saloon offering a Free Lunch served a hot dish at noon, another at five o'clock, and a final meal at midnight.

The Harquette Brothers' Palace of Art opulent Saloon and Restaurant at 16 Post Street was a unique example of the higher class of eating and drinking establishments on the Cocktail Route. Because it was to be expected that behavior would be reasonably decorous, this particular saloon was not as popular with the "top nobs" as other, rowdier eateries. Ladies were attracted by the saloon's artistic display of fine paintings, marble carvings, lovely silver cups and other silver objects, cast-iron statuary, curios, and wooden *objets d'art*, and so it became necessary for gentlemen to restrain themselves from the usual alcoholic exuberance of the Route. Despite the fact that most of the oil paintings were of nude females in various sublime poses, surprisingly, the Palace of Art remained a favorite with women. Visitors to San Francisco were astounded by the accessibility of the free feasts even when the patron spent only five cents for a schooner of beer. Unfortunately, the Palace of Art itself and all its treasures were lost in the Great Fire of 1906. But the traditional free lunch continued to appear elsewhere in the city until the early 1920s.

PALACE OF ART SALOON BAKED HAM

1 premium quality 5-pound canned ham
½ cup tarragon vinegar
½ cup loosely packed brown sugar
1 teaspoon prepared mustard
1 teaspoon ground cloves
¼ teaspoon nutmeg
Whole cloves, to cook's touch
Number 16 Post Street Ham Sauce
Palace of Art Saloon Spiced Apricots, for garnish

Preheat oven to 350 degrees F. In a baking dish that has a cover, pour the vinegar over the ham and its juices. Mix together the brown sugar, mustard, ground cloves, and nutmeg, and pat on the ham. Decorate the ham with the whole cloves, then bake it, covered, 15 minutes for each pound of ham. Baste the meat occasionally with its juices. Serve the ham sliced with Number 16 Post Street Ham Sauce and a garnish of Spiced Apricots. SERVES 6 AS AN ENTRÉE.

NUMBER 16 POST STREET HAM SAUCE

1 cup brown sugar
2 teaspoons arrowroot
¼ teaspoon dry mustard
¼ teaspoon ground cloves
¼ teaspoon allspice
¼ teaspoon cinnamon
½ teaspoon salt
1 cup seedless white raisins
½ cup tarragon vinegar
2 cups light dry red wine
¼ cup salad oil
2 tablespoons melted butter

Mix together all the dry ingredients in a double boiler. Mix the liquid ingredients together. Then blend the liquid ingredients into the dry ones and cook the sauce over simmering water, stirring, just until it is thickened and the raisins are plump.

PALACE OF ART FREE LUNCH MENU   (OVERLEAF)

The Palace of Art.

COMMERCIAL LUNCH MENU

FROM 11 TO 2:30

LUNCH, INCLUDING PLAIN DRINK, 25 CTS.

Soup.

Mock Turtle   Ox Tail   Chicken Gumbo

Entrees.

Fish   Veal Patti   Roggue

Roast.

Beef   Mutton   Pork   Leg of Lamb

Vegetables.

Potatoes   Cauliflower   Tomatoes

Cheese   Cafe Noir.

Extras.

Radishes   Celery   Crab Salad

PLEASE PAY THE WAITER

Any Inattention, Impoliteness or Overcharges on the part of
the Employees, please report to the Management.

The Palace of Art.

OUR FREE LUNCH.

Served with All Drinks, from 4 to 11 P. M.

Radishes	Crab Salad	Celery

Clam Juice

Pigs Head	Bolinas Bay Clams	Head Cheese
Saucisses à la Famille		Beef à la Chile Colorado
Chili Con Carne		Honolulu Beans
Chicken Croquette	Veal Croquette	Terrapin Stew
Fried Clams	Sardines	Boiled Ham
Saratoga Chips		Corned Beef
Cold Tongue	Beef Stew	Pork and Beans
Chipped Beef		Smoked Salmon
Cheese		Crackers
Cracked Crab		Holland Herring
Almonds	Pop Corn	Apples

FOR WINE LIST SEE LAST PAGE.

PALACE OF ART SALOON SPICED APRICOTS

1 (2½-pound) can whole apricots, with 1 cup of the liquid
5 tablespoons brown sugar
2 teaspoons allspice
¼ teaspoon nutmeg
1 tablespoon butter

Simmer the fruit in a syrup of the remaining ingredients until the liquid is reduced by half. Chill. May be used as a garnish for veal as well as ham.

To make spiced peaches, substitute canned cling peaches for the apricots.

San Francisco had its own style of the popular Waldorf salad, much in vogue during the days of the Free Lunch. When baked ham is left over, dice the meat for this delicious version:

COCKTAIL ROUTE WALDORF SALAD WITH HAM

2 oranges
2 cups diced ham
1 cup diced peeled apples
½ cup diced celery
½ cup diced walnuts
¼ cup minced onion
½ cup white raisins
½ cup mayonnaise
2 tablespoons milk
1 teaspoon Worcestershire sauce
Pepper to cook's taste
Lettuce leaves
½ teaspoon paprika

Peel the oranges and remove the membrane from the sections over a bowl to catch the juice. Set aside 1 tablespoon of the juice and as many orange sections as you'll have salad servings. Drain the remaining oranges, reserving the juice, and combine them with the ham, diced apples, celery, walnuts, onion, and raisins, in a bowl. In a separate bowl, blend well the mayonnaise, milk, and reserved orange juice. Add the Worcestershire sauce and pepper, and again stir the dressing thoroughly. Pour it over the salad mixture, tossing lightly, and serve the salad over crisp lettuce leaves. Garnish the individual servings with orange slices sprinkled with paprika, for a dash of unexpected color. SERVES 6 TO 8.

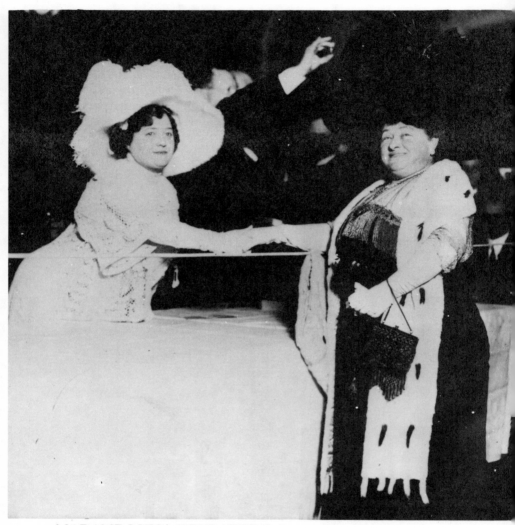

MADAME LUISA TETRAZZINI, in an ermine wrap,
before the start of her Christmas Eve concert
Photo courtesy of the California Historical Society, San Francisco

For Luisa Tetrazzini

Beloved Mother-Figure to a Musical City

Luisa Tetrazzini, the coloratura soprano, enchanted the San Francisco of her day, though not for the magic of her voice or for the meandering proportions of her bountiful figure. The great diva looked like everybody's loving, stout, good-natured mother, and San Franciscans took her to their hearts as a lady who obviously loved to eat well, was completely Italian, and seemed to overflow with amiable good spirits. Earlier, when a San Francisco opera director found the proud woman impoverished and nearly down-and-out in Mexico and rescued her from oblivion, he could not have possibly known that he had discovered a singer destined for international glory. But no matter what the rest of the world thought of her, Tetrazzini carried on a love affair with this city that never ended. In any other town, creating a chicken dish to honor a performer might have been taken for a modest gesture, but not so in San Francisco. Here, where appreciation for great singing and for great cuisine were inseparable, it was the supreme tribute.

CHICKEN TETRAZZINI

6 pounds stewing chicken, in pieces
1 white onion, sliced
2 stalks of celery
Salt to taste
1 bay leaf
3 cups water
½ cup + ½ cup butter
½ cup flour
¼ teaspoon dried red pepper
½ pound fresh mushrooms, sliced
1 egg yolk, beaten

1 tablespoon dry sherry
3 tablespoons heavy cream
8 ounces uncooked spaghetti
Imported Parmesan cheese, grated, to cook's touch

Place the chicken pieces, onion, celery, a little salt, the bay leaf, and the water in a heavy casserole. After bringing the liquid to a boil, reduce the heat and let the chicken simmer until it is tender. Strain the broth, reserving it; discard the vegetables and skin and bone the chicken. Cut the meat into cubes.

In a separate saucepan over a very low heat, melt ½ cup of the butter and slowly add the flour and a little salt, stirring constantly for about 5 minutes. Then add 2 cups of the clear broth to the flour mixture, continuing to stir until the sauce is thickened and completely smooth. Mix in the red pepper.

In a separate skillet, quickly sauté the mushrooms in 2 tablespoons of the remaining ½ cup of butter. Then stir into the simmering sauce the beaten egg yolk, sherry, cream, the drained mushrooms, and the chicken cubes. Simmer these gently. Do not let the sauce boil. A little more red pepper may be added, to taste.

Cook the spaghetti according to the directions on the package, *al dente*. Drain the pasta. Alternate layers of the spaghetti, the sauce, and some of the Parmesan cheese in a buttered heatproof casserole, ending with the sauce and a liberal amount of the cheese. Dot the casserole with the remaining butter. Quickly brown the top in a preheated broiler. Serve with a light, dry Italian white wine.
SERVES 6 AS AN ENTRÉE.

For Nellie Melba
Partly the World's and Partly Our Own

The Australian songbird, Nellie Melba, was noted for two things other than her voice: She habitually broke men's hearts, and she inspired culinary artists to create dishes and drinks that would forever carry her name. Melba was not as beloved in San Francisco as the motherly Tetrazzini, but she appeared so often in the city that it must have seemed like a second home to her. Her constant appearances, both in concerts and in fine restaurants, conspired to make her a real San Franciscan. Unfortunately, behind her public image, Melba carefully hid a particularly nasty temper. But when she was wined and dined by her many gentlemen friends in the majestic Red Room at the Bohemian Club, dear Nellie could radiate superb sparkle and wit. Perhaps she may have been an ill-tempered serpent smuggled unknowingly into the Bohemian gardens, but her great redeeming social feature was that she doted on all the sensual pleasures and fully expected to receive all of them. No sensual San Franciscan male could possibly resist such a challenge. Presumably, few did.

Although Peach Melba was not invented in San Francisco, the better restaurants vied with each other to serve the best rendition. The classic recipe, still to be found in nearly every cookbook, requires a ripened peach half to be filled with a scoop of vanilla ice cream and topped with a sauce of mixed raspberries and currant jelly simmered in water and cornstarch until clear.

Melba Fizz was probably first served in our town. At the time the drink made its appearance, gin was just coming into its own and was considered "fast," which meant it was not for "nice girls." Whatever else, Melba was certainly no prude. We should be eternally grateful to the diva that she made gin quite fashionable in San Francisco!

71

MADAME NELLIE MELBA, as Marguerite in *Faust*
Photo courtesy of the California Historical Society, San Francisco

FIZZ MELBA

1½ ounces gin
1 ounce lemon juice
1 egg white
½ ounce currant syrup
½ cup cracked ice

Whip the first 4 ingredients in an electric blender for 10 to 15 seconds. Pour the fizz over cracked ice in a prechilled 8-ounce glass. SERVES 1.

Melba was consistent in another area, too. She periodically retired. In fact, her critics said she "retired" more than she "appeared." A young Englishman, Beverly Nichols, was lured to Australia to become her secretary and, later, to ghost-write her autobiography. Their relationship soon erupted into a blistering feud. Nichols, who then wrote a fictional biography of the soprano under the title of *Evensong*, published in 1932, satirized Melba as "Madame Irela," who made more make-believe farewell appearances than did the real-life diva in her later years.

Nellie Melba came out of one of her many retirements in San Francisco with these immortal words: "I feel it is my duty!" Meanwhile, Nichols had penned several stinging lines which appear in a copy of the novel from a private collection:

Oh, the futility of words, of
printed words, that flutter like
dead leaves in the breath of that voice!

Here is a long-buried recipe in honor of Nellie Melba discovered in the files of a San Francisco home economist:

BREAST OF CHICKEN MELBA

3 chicken breasts
Salt to taste
Cayenne pepper to taste
½ cup + 2 tablespoons butter
½ cup + 1 tablespoon dry white wine
½ cup raw, sliced mushrooms

½ cup seedless white grapes
1 cup heavy cream
3 slices of toast

Preheat oven to 350 degrees F. Bone and skin the 3 chicken breasts, and season them with salt and cayenne pepper. Sauté them in ½ cup of the butter. When the meat is golden on both sides, stir in the 2 tablespoons of butter and ½ cup of the dry white wine. In a tightly covered baking dish that later can be used on the stove, bake the chicken for 25 minutes. Then add the sliced mushrooms and the white grapes. Add the remaining tablespoon of dry white wine, and, on top of the stove, simmer the dish uncovered for 10 minutes. Add the heavy cream and simmer the chicken for an additional 5 minutes. Serve it piping hot on the toast, which has been dipped in the sauce. SERVES 3.

Pisco Punch
Or the Perfect Paralyzer

The insidious Pisco Punch was invented by a Scotsman, Duncan Nichol, who dispensed it liberally from his own bar, the famous Bank Exchange Saloon, which occupied one corner of the massive Montgomery Block near the downtown section of the old Barbary Coast. This discriminating water hole, originally founded by John Torrence and George Parker (the latter of the hotel family fame), was put out of business by the destructing force of Prohibition. But the site will live forever as the birthplace of the most lethal alcoholic bomb ever conceived by man.

Beginning in the 1870s, Pisco Punch was the most popular drink in town. Nichol's private recipe was often imitated but never equaled; its secret died with him. The base for the potent punch was Pisco brandy distilled from the Italian grape, or *la rosa del Peru*. Pisco was the name of the Peruvian port from which it was shipped to San Francisco. Thomas W. Knox said, in *Underground, or Life Below the Surface:* "It is perfectly colorless, quite fragrant, very seductive, terribly strong, and has a flavor somewhat resembling Scotch whiskey, but much more delicate, with a marked fruity taste. It comes in earthen jars holding about five gallons each. We had some hot, with a bit of lemon and a dash of nutmeg in it. The first glass satisfied me that San Francisco was, and is, a nice place to visit. The second glass was sufficient, and I felt I could face smallpox, all the fevers known to the faculty, and the Asiatic cholera combined, if need be."

At the turn of the century, it became too expensive to transport the liquor from Peru, so a brandy from St. Helena, California, in the Napa Valley was substituted. Nearly any brandy would have sufficed, however. We substitute this version of the punch for Nichol's:

75

PISCO PUNCH

1 tablespoon Pernod
1¼ ounces Pisco Peruvian or other brandy
1 ounce Meyer's catawba or any grape juice
Shaved ice
6 ounces chilled pineapple juice

Coat the inside of an ample fizz glass with Pernod by swirling the liquor around the glass. Discard any of the liquid that does not cling. Pour the brandy into the glass and add the grape juice. Fill the glass with shaved ice and pour chilled pineapple juice to the brim. SERVES 1.

Pisco Punch was not the only secret in Duncan Nichol's head. He also served something called Button Punch, again with a Pisco base. Rudyard Kipling, often critical of San Francisco, waxed lyrical over Button Punch. Commenting in his *From Sea to Sea*, which was published in 1899, Kipling wrote: "It is the highest and noblest product of the age. I have a theory it is compounded of cherub's wings, the glory of a tropical dawn, the red clouds of sunset, and the fragments of lost epics by dead masters." Hail to thee, Pisco!

DUNCAN NICHOL, with three "pals" and the staff
of his Bank Exchange at the turn of the century
Photo courtesy of the California Section, California State Library

Birds of a Feather and Some Others

At the century's turn, Charles F. Lummis, California's first librarian, found himself in charge of The Landmarks Club, a statewide organization formed to preserve historic buildings. To raise funds, Lummis edited and published *The Landmarks Club Cook Book* in 1903, and included a dozen of his personal recipes. We have re-created three of them since they were inspired by San Francisco where drunken pigeons, beautiful mulattoes, and coveys of quail were taken for granted, then and now.

PICHONES BORRACHOS
"Drunken Pigeons"

4 small squabs
6 medium tomatoes
Toasted almonds, slivered, to cook's touch
1 clove garlic
1 pint red cooking wine
⅓ cup dark raisins
Peels of 3 slices lemon
1 cup pitted ripe olives
1 teaspoon sugar
¼ teaspoon cinnamon
Freshly ground pepper to taste
1 whole clove
Fresh parsley, for garnish

Stew the squabs until nearly done and remove from the pan. Peel the tomatoes and add to the pan juices along with the almonds. Add the garlic, cooking wine, raisins, lemon peel, olives, sugar, cinnamon, pepper, and clove. Return the squabs to the pan and cook until done. Garnish with fresh parsley. SERVES 4 AS AN ENTRÉE.

POLLO DE LA BELLA MULATA
"Chickens à la Beautiful Mulatta"

2 small frying chickens, cut in pieces
¼ cup + ¼ cup olive oil
1 large onion, chopped
4 medium tomatoes, diced
½ cup finely chopped almonds
½ teaspoon salt
Freshly ground pepper to taste
1 whole clove
1 cup very dry sherry
Fresh parsley sprigs, for garnish

In a large skillet, sauté the chicken pieces in ¼ cup olive oil until golden brown and fully cooked. In another skillet, sauté the chopped onion in ¼ cup of olive oil until golden but not brown. Add the tomatoes to the onions and then add the almonds, salt, pepper, and clove. Cook until the tomatoes are tender and then add the chicken and sherry to this mixture. Bring to a boil. Arrange chicken pieces with the sauce on a hot platter. Garnish with fresh parsley. SERVES 4 AS AN ENTRÉE.

SMOTHERED QUAIL
"Our Perky, Petulant State Bird"

4 small quail
Flour
Salt and pepper to taste
Butter
4 slices of toast

Preheat oven to 370 degrees F. Split each quail up the back, rub all over with flour, salt, and pepper. Then butter each bird. Bake ½ hour in a covered pan with enough water to keep the fowl from burning. When done, remove the quail from the pan and make a gravy of the remaining juices by adding a little flour. Serve each bird on toast with the gravy poured over it. SERVES 4 AS AN ENTRÉE.

In the 1900s, quail were considered pests. Today, the delightful little creatures are a protected species and have the run of Golden Gate Park.

IV.
WHERE THEY DINED SUPERBLY
BY GASLIGHT

THE POODLE DOG RESTAURANT, on Bush Street
Photo courtesy of the California Section, California State Library

The Poodle Dog

The Greatest French Restaurant of the Golden Era

It seems as if there has always been a Poodle Dog restaurant, under one guise or another, in the downtown area. Started by a French chef from New Orleans in 1849, the first establishment was called the Poule d'Or, and was situated at Clay and Dupont (now Grant Avenue). In 1868, when it was moved to the corner of Bush and Grant into a multistoried building, its name was formally changed to the Poodle Dog Restaurant. Toward the end of the century, Calixte Lalanne became *chef de cuisine* and brought the Poodle Dog to the height of its culinary creativity. This location was completely destroyed in 1906; Chef Lalanne acquired new partners and rebuilt the restaurant on Bush Street in 1908, where it flourished until Prohibition. In 1933, it reopened as the Ritz French Restaurant, and in the 1940s, Calixte Lalanne's son, Louis, renamed the place the Ritz Old Poodle Dog. While it is a bit of a muddle to keep track of the various changes in names, partners, and locations, this restaurant was the major influence of French *haute cuisine* in San Francisco during the golden years. And in 1984 a new Poodle Dog opened its doors in the city.

Shortly after the Great Fire, George Brauer, one of Lalanne's protégés in the kitchen, defected to Blanco's Restaurant. He took to his new establishment the secret of the Poodle Dog's most famous recipe, Frog Legs Poulette, and thereby a legendary dish has at least been partly saved from oblivion. This recipe survived with oysters substituted for frog legs:

OYSTERS à LA POULETTE

½ cup butter
3 tablespoons flour
1 teaspoon salt
Dash of white pepper
1 generous tablespoon lemon juice

83

2 cups chicken or veal stock
3 egg yolks
2 dozen large oysters, removed from shells

Combine the ingredients, except the oysters, and pour into the top
of a double boiler. First drain and then stir in the oysters, and let
them cook until the edges curl up. Serve hot. SERVES 4 AS AN ENTRÉE.

The Poodle Dog in its heyday offered five levels of pure pleasure.
The first floor of the building housed the family restaurant, and the
second floor was decorated for lavish banquets. The top three floors
were reached by means of a side entrance and private birdcage eleva-
tor. These special floors contained some very sumptuous suites, and
wealthy patrons could easily indulge themselves secretly in whatever
whims caught their fancy. Despite its reputation as a discreet place
for hidden rendezvous, the Poodle Dog remained quite free from
public scandal. Only a few alleged tales of impropriety were ever
whispered, and the proud owners managed to keep its name unsullied
from vulgar accusations.

The partners of Bergez's, Frank's, and the Old Poodle Dog eventually merged to form one restaurant. Charles Schmitt was the chef.
Because he shared one of his most elegant recipes with Sperry Products to advance the sales of the flour, this Poodle Dog dessert soufflé
has been preserved and can be duplicated.

SOUFFLÉ ROTHSCHILD

2 tablespoons butter
2 tablespoons + 2 teaspoons sugar
8 macaroons
Brandy, to cook's touch
½ cup milk
1 tablespoon flour
3 eggs, separated
1 ounce glacé fruit, chopped into small pieces
½ ounce semisweet chocolate, grated

Preheat oven to 350 degrees F. Rub a tablespoon of the butter inside a medium-sized soufflé mold and sprinkle it with a teaspoon of sugar. Crumble the macaroons into a little brandy, and let them soak for several minutes. Boil half the milk with 2 tablespoons of the sugar. Dissolve the flour in the remaining cold milk, add this to the boiled milk, and cook it for 2 minutes. Remove the milk from the heat to cool before adding the egg yolks, thoroughly beaten. Bring this mixture to a slight boil, then remove it from the heat. Beat the whites of the eggs and the remaining teaspoonful of sugar until stiff peaks form, and fold them into the warm soufflé mixture. Then, in quick steps, pour half of it into the mold and top it with the fruit pieces, crumbled macaroons, and grated chocolate; pour in the rest of the soufflé mixture and slide it into preheated oven. Bake the soufflé for 25 minutes and serve it at once. SERVES 4 AS A DESSERT.

COPPA'S RESTAURANT, in the Montgomery Block, which
featured a central mural with the famous Seth Thomas wall clock
Photo courtesy of the California Section, California State Library

Coppa's

The Favorite of Convivial Bohemia

Coppa's was San Francisco's first truly Bohemian restaurant. Joseph
Coppa came to the city from Turin, Italy, by way of Paris and Guate-
mala. Before opening his first tiny restaurant in North Beach, he
had cooked at such elegant establishments as Martinelli's and the
Poodle Dog. He was also chef at the Occidental Hotel. In the 1900s,
his persuasive friend O. P. Stidger convinced Coppa he should move
to the prestigious Montgomery Block, the giant structure at the corner
of Montgomery and Merchant streets. Stidger wanted Coppa to oc-
cupy the Merchant Street corner, and the chef agreed to the location.
Stidger thought the restaurant would be an excellent companion to
Duncan Nichol's Bank Exchange Saloon, which was housed in another corner of the huge building. The narrow, high-ceilinged quarters rented by Coppa had room for about twenty tables, with space
in the back near the kitchen for an overflow crowd. Since "The Block"
was the bastion of local Bohemia, Coppa's at once attracted a fascinating literary and artistic clientele. More than the food, it was Poppa
Coppa's warm smile and generous heart that brought in his often
penniless customers.

The restaurant gave rise to what became known as Coppa's School
of Literature, a group of hard drinkers and high rollers who gained
most of their inspirations from the plentiful supply of "Table Red."
After the Montgomery Block was badly damaged in 1906, Coppa tried
his hand at several new restaurants, one being the Neptune Palace
at the corner of Kearny and Jackson streets. Finally, he opened Coppa's Pompeiian Garden, outside the then city limits on the road to
San Mateo. He retired in the late 1930s in his eighth decade.

But nothing ever matched or replaced the glorious heydays in "The
Block." George Sterling, Jack London, Will Irwin, Gelett Burgess,
Maynard Dixon, Xavier Martinez—London's artist pal—and many
other Bohemians frequented the place. And the present-day Bohemian
Club had its origins at Coppa's tables. Jack London and Anna Strunsky

wrote a good part of the *Kempton-Wace Letters* inside Coppa's doors. Porter Garnett, an authentic *bon vivant*, was one of Poppa Coppa's most faithful regulars. In later years, Garnett was a leading figure of the Bohemian Club, and he wrote some of the best chronicles of its history.

It was not really just the food that gave Coppa's its bold flavor, nor was it the colorful folk whom uptowners dubbed "artistes." Rather, it was the totally original decorations with which the entire wall space of the restaurant was covered. When Coppa repainted his walls a ghastly shade of red, Garnett and the other Bohemians persuaded him to let them cover the hideous color with inspirational murals. The designs included a frieze within which were written the names of those thought worthy of Bohemia's Hall of Fame. The prosaic name of "Maisie" between those of Goethe and Nietzsche stood for a well-known San Francisco newspaperwoman. The unlikely name of "Buttsky" was a tribute to another lady much favored by the regulars. Xavier "Marty" Martinez painted a line of prowling black cats above the frieze, which extended around all sides of the room. Martinez, a Mexican artist thought to be "exotic," had just returned from six years in Paris. At the time Jack London was frequenting Coppa's, Martinez became one of his closest and dearest friends. To add luster to the total effect, Porter Garnett painted the walls with quotations from the philosophers, mixed with those of the Coppa Bohemians. Sadly, only photographs survive to recall the lost glory of the Coppa murals.

The following recipe was named for Don Gaspar de Pórtola, first governor of the Californias. Coppa considered it his supreme masterpiece: "Ah, Chicken Pórtola. That is my own idea. It is the most delicious way chicken was ever cooked!"

JOSEPH COPPA'S CHICKEN PÓRTOLA

    1 fresh coconut
    1 (12-ounce) can corn kernels, drained
    2 medium onions, chopped
    4 tablespoons olive oil
    1 green pepper, chopped
    1 tablespoon diced, broiled bacon

6 tomatoes, chopped
1 clove garlic, diced
Salt and pepper to taste
½ large frying chicken, cut into 4 pieces

Preheat oven to 350 degrees F. Cut the top off the coconut, and remove nearly all the meat. Chop the coconut meat into small pieces, combine with corn kernels, and reserve the mixture. Sauté the onions in olive oil; when they are golden, add the green pepper, bacon, tomatoes, and garlic. Cook these ingredients until they are blended and thick. Add the corn and coconut pieces and season mixture with salt and pepper. Add the chicken parts, and spoon the whole into the coconut shell. Close as tightly as possible with top of the shell. Prop the coconut in a pan filled with hot water and set in the preheated oven for 1 hour. Baste the coconut shell with water occasionally; watch that the water in the outside pan does not evaporate. When the chicken is thoroughly cooked through and is tender when forked, serve it in the shell of the coconut. SERVES—only the daring!

ABE WARNER and some of his "regulars" at his Cobweb Palace
in North Beach
Photo courtesy of the California Section, California State Library

Monkey Warner's Cobweb Palace
The Oddest Place in Town

For forty-one years, the most colorful and unique saloon in town was Abe Warner's Cobweb Palace, on Meiggs Wharf in North Beach. A former sailor, Warner founded the place in 1856 and kept it going until 1897, when he retired at the age of eighty. The ramshackle shed was a favorite with sailors, who brought Warner all kinds of souvenirs. The place was crammed to the rafters with such items as warclubs from the Pacific, oriental masks, live animals including monkeys, parrots, magpies, and other exotic birds, bolos, an Eskimo canoe, a totem pole, a complete set of dentures that had once belonged to a sperm whale, and many rude paintings of many rude women! This grotesque conglomeration was left to molder under an undisturbed network of cobwebs because Warner had a great fondness for spiders and he simply refused to disturb their natural habits.

Warner allowed cats, dogs, and even bears to roam his saloon at will, much to the delight of children who came with their fathers to see the menagerie. Herbert Asbury writes that one parrot, which had the run of the place, could curse bountifully in four languages and sometimes hailed Warner as "Grandpa" when the besotted bird had imbibed not too wisely but too well! Only the freshest seafood was served at the Cobweb Palace with many varieties on the menu. The bar at the end of the shed, reached by climbing over and around the relics, was stocked with the finest brandies, rarest wines, and most expensive liquors and potents to be found anywhere in the city. Despite the surroundings, Warner catered to a class of men who knew good liquors. It was their habit to top off a superb fish dinner with one of Warner's fine French brandies. Regardless of the clutter and the grime and the dust of ages, Warner never served his patrons anything but the finest!

The States

The Pedestrian Abalone,
Or How It Was Rescued from Oblivion

The States Restaurant had a curious history. First opened in 1907 on Ellis Street by Henry Hirsch, it was then called the Heidelberg Inn. In 1912, the restaurant moved to new quarters at Market and Fourth streets under the name of Hof Brau. Just before the Great War, the proprietor prudently added the name "The States." Hirsch even engraved the different names of the states of the Union over the dining booths. But, at heart, the restaurant remained a hof brau; it was still a great place to eat German food and drink draft beer. The huge basement was divided into a series of decorative dining rooms with distinct themes such as the Apple Orchard, Indian Grill, Oriental Grill, and the Hunting Lodge. This was a strange conglomeration to be mixed with the names of the various states.

The States scored a first in San Francisco when it shipped frozen reindeer meat from Alaska, offering the expensive entrée as "Alaska Reindeer Steak." The States did not survive the repression of Prohibition, however. The restaurant that reopened after Repeal, in another basement at Market and Eddy streets, had only theme and name in common with the old establishment.

But before the dire advent of the Volstead Act, Chef "Pop" Ernst etched the name of the house forever in the culinary annals of San Francisco when he tarted-up the common abalone and rescued it from an undeserving fate as a drab, ignominious nonentity. Ernst discovered that if he pounded the confounded thing just enough, dredged it in flour and eggs, and then fried it correctly, the unpalatable and embarrassed abalone became a delicious morsel fit for any king. Chef Ernst did not rescue the abalone entirely out of the goodness of his heart, however. He was motivated purely for profit—and how the money began to roll in! The improbable delicacy ensured the prosperity of The States until the ban of alcoholic beverages in 1920. Today, Chef Ernst would surely roll in his grave if he knew that the best abalone obtainable in any restaurant in America is not served in San

The States Restaurant
SAN FRANCISCO
"APPLE ORCHARD"

THE STATES RESTAURANT, "Apple Orchard" Room
Photo courtesy of the California Historical Society, San Francisco

Francisco. Rather, it is featured at Nicola's Restaurant in the heart of a downtown section of Los Angeles near Dodger Stadium. While he would undoubtedly disapprove of the location, he would have enthusiastically praised the dish, as the Nicola twins use virtually the same recipe invented by Ernst.

Abalone is not frequently prepared at home. Nevertheless, you might like to try Chef Ernst's successful technique. After cutting away the dark portion, slice the abalone against the grain into pieces about ½ inch thick. Pound the pieces continuously with a light but steady hand. (Like veal, abalone will "break down" if pounded too hard.) Prepare 2 bowls, one with flour seasoned with salt and pepper, and the other containing milk and 2 beaten eggs. After dipping the pieces of abalone first into the milk and then into the seasoned flour, quickly sauté the pieces 20 seconds per side in a frying pan coated with hot olive oil. Overcooking makes abalone as tough as shoe leather, so a careless cook gets a rude surprise.

Today, it is common to find abalone dressed with lemon slices, overflowing with parsley, and sometimes even drenched with almonds. Abalone at The States was served simply and unadorned, with a heaping dish of creamy tartar sauce. Since tartar sauce is the only perfect accompaniment for Chef Ernst's masterpiece, we have included this turn-of-the-century recipe from the treasured *S&W Greenbook of Recipes*.

HOMEMADE TARTAR SAUCE

    1 raw egg yolk
    1 teaspoon dry mustard
    1 teaspoon salt
    Dash cayenne pepper
    3 tablespoons lemon juice or vinegar
    ½ cup olive oil
    1 teaspoon chopped fresh parsley
    1 teaspoon capers
    1 teaspoon chopped gherkins
    1 teaspoon finely minced onions

Blend with a wooden spoon the egg yolk, mustard, salt, and as much cayenne pepper "as can be taken on the point of a small penknife," or about ⅛ teaspoon. Then add, a few drops at a time, stirring quickly and continuously, the lemon juice or vinegar and the olive oil. When the sauce has become thick and smooth, add the chopped parsley, capers, gherkins, and onion. Keep the sauce cool until served.

An unusual side dish for the abalone is the *Greenbook*'s version of Saratoga Potatoes—an eighty-year-old recipe for potato chips. This recipe again proves there is really nothing new under the sun—even San Francisco's elusive sun.

SARATOGA POTATOES

Number of potatoes desired
Olive oil to cover a few slices
Salt to taste

Pare and slice the potatoes very thin, and drop the slices into cold water. Drain them, and dry them well in a towel. Fry a few at a time in hot olive oil. Drain the potatoes on paper towels, and add salt to taste.

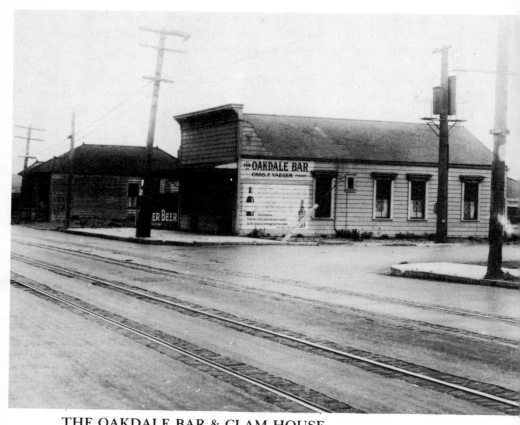

THE OAKDALE BAR & CLAM HOUSE
Photo courtesy of the California Section, California State Library

The Oakdale Bar

Home of San Francisco's Own Style of Clam Chowder

The Oakdale Bar & Clam House, opened in 1861 and for many years established at the corner of Oakdale and San Bruno avenues, was considered responsible for the meteoric rise of the local clam from obscurity to prominence in the Gaslight Era. San Francisco's own style of clam chowder, neither Boston nor Manhattan, but "Golden Gate," might have originated in this restaurant.

SAN FRANCISCO CLAM CHOWDER

4 slices of bacon, diced
2 yellow onions, chopped
6 green onions, chopped
1 tablespoon dried parsley
2 small potatoes, peeled and diced
1 tablespoon chopped chervil
1 cup chopped celery
½ teaspoon dried thyme
1 cup water
Salt and freshly ground pepper to taste
2 (8-ounce) cans chopped or minced clams, with their juice
¼ cube butter
1½ cups milk

In a large, heavy casserole, sauté the bacon until it is crisp, and reserve it. Discard all but 2 tablespoons of the drippings. Add to this the yellow onions and cook them until golden, then stir in the green onions, parsley, potatoes, chervil, celery, thyme, water, and some salt and pepper. Add the juice from the clams, reserving the clams. Cover and cook the soup until the potatoes are tender. Then add the butter, clams, and milk. Heat the soup until it is steaming. Garnish with the bacon and serve it with oyster crackers. SERVES 6.

THE GIANDUJA RESTAURANT
Photo courtesy of the California Historical Society, San Francisco

Brenti's La Gianduja

The Best Thirty-five-cent Lunch in North Beach

"Zhan-du-ya" was the proper way to pronounce the name of the best lunch spot in the uninhibited section of town known as North Beach. Good cooking and excellent service were the prime reasons to make the trip to the end of Stockton Street at Washington Square. La Gianduja featured peasant-style meals, but it also offered a wide range of more elaborate dishes. However, the customers' favorite entrée was the unpretentious, humble but delicious pot roast, which was served with a particularly virile Italian grape brandy called Grappa.

THE THIRTY-FIVE-CENT PEASANT POT ROAST

4 to 6 pounds beef top round or chuck
1 lemon, sliced
5 cloves garlic, crushed
1 teaspoon dried thyme
1 teaspoon dried oregano
2 bay leaves
1 teaspoon dried tarragon
Pepper to taste
2 cups dry red wine
½ cup imported olive oil
4 slices of bacon
5 fresh tomatoes, sliced
1 tablespoon dried parsley
1 cup beef stock
4 shallots, minced
Salt to taste
6 small peeled white onions, whole
1 pound mushrooms, sliced
Fresh parsley sprigs, for garnish
Flour or arrowroot

Pour over the beef in a large bowl a marinade of the lemon, garlic, thyme, oregano, bay leaves, tarragon, pepper, red wine, and olive oil. Cover the bowl and refrigerate it for at least 12 hours, turning the meat from time to time.

Preheat oven to 300 degrees F. In a heavy pan or Dutch oven place the bacon and the meat with its marinade. Add the tomatoes, parsley, beef stock, shallots, and a little salt and pepper, and cover the pan tightly. Cook the meat about 5 hours or until it is just tender. Add the onions and mushrooms. Again cover the pan and cook the meat for another hour. Then remove the meat to a hot platter, garnish it with the cooked onions, mushrooms, and plentiful sprigs of parsley, and keep it warm while thickening the juices with arrowroot or flour as a gravy for the pot roast. SERVES 6 TO 8 AS AN ENTRÉE.

Bonini's Barn

The Pleasures of the South-Italian Style

In the heart of North Beach, near the intersection of Washington and Columbus streets, Bonini's Barn was strictly "Italian Country," where the smoke from dry twisted black cigars wafted over the heads of its habitués, who sat drinking Amer Picon, eating cheese that really came from Parma, and playing endless games of pangini. It didn't matter that the food was probably better somewhere down the street or that the room looked like a barnyard, complete with chickens and pigeons strutting around and sometimes even jumping on the tables. What did matter was that Bonini's was comfortable, and it was fun. Most of the dishes served in this improbable restaurant were cooked with tomato-based sauces, strictly southern Italian style. Here's a dandy that is as Italian as if it sprang from the center of Naples itself. *Mangiari e piaceri!*

MEAT SAUCE VESUVIUS

1 large onion, chopped
½ cup cooking oil
1 bottle of catsup
1½ cups water or dry red wine
6 tablespoons Worcestershire sauce
3 tablespoons powdered mustard
1 teaspoon freshly ground black pepper
1 teaspoon salt
1 teaspoon chili powder
3 heaping tablespoons brown sugar
3 teaspoons red wine vinegar
Juice of 1 large lemon

BONINI'S BARN in North Beach
Photo courtesy of the California Historical Society, San Francisco

Partially cook the onions in the oil, then add all the ingredients and simmer for 1 hour. If it thickens too much, thin it from time to time with more water or red wine. Do not double this recipe; the sauce never tastes the same when the portions are increased, though why this should be is a mystery. The sauce will keep for weeks in the refrigerator. This one lifts ordinary meats to new glory.

Bonini's also served a simple but rich meat sauce for pasta:

PASTA SAUCE MOUNT ETNA

3 tablespoons olive oil
1 pound hot Italian sausage, crumbled
1 pound extra-lean ground beef
1 large yellow onion, chopped
3 cloves garlic, chopped or pressed
3 (8-ounce) cans tomato sauce
1½ cups dry red wine
½ teaspoon dried basil
½ teaspoon dried oregano
½ teaspoon dried thyme
½ teaspoon dried rosemary
1 teaspoon sugar
Salt to taste
Freshly ground black pepper to taste
Dash of Tabasco sauce
Italian cheese, finely grated, to cook's touch

Heat the oil in large, heavy skillet or Dutch oven; add the sausage, beef, onion, and garlic. Cook over medium heat, stirring frequently until the meat is nicely browned. Add tomato sauce, red wine, basil, oregano, thyme, rosemary, sugar, salt, pepper, and Tabasco and mix them thoroughly with the other ingredients. Cover the sauce and simmer very gently for 1 hour, stirring occasionally. Serve piping hot over pasta and sprinkle with Italian cheese of the cook's choice. SERVES 6 OVER PASTA AS AN ENTRÉE.

THE OLD TADICH GRILL
Photo courtesy of the San Francisco Archives, San Francisco Public Library

Tadich Grill
The Original "Cold Day" Restaurant

Tadich Grill on California Street, which dates back to 1849, is among the oldest existing restaurants in California. Despite the anonymous couplet, "Blessed are those who live by the Bay—one day they are hot, the next day they are not," in this case "Cold Day" has nothing to do with our weather. Alexander Badlam, a politician of the nineties, celebrated an election victory and was heard to remark, "It's a cold day when I get left!" It was thought that he might have made this comment at the Tadich Grill, so the restaurant was stuck with "Cold Day" as part of its historical name. We have included a hot recipe for a typical cool San Francisco day:

CALIFORNIA STREET HOT POTATO SALAD

4 slices of bacon
1 tablespoon flour
1 tablespoon sugar
½ teaspoon salt
Freshly ground black pepper to taste, if desired
½ teaspoon celery seeds
1 teaspoon dry mustard
Garlic, to cook's touch, minced
½ cup water
¼ cup cider vinegar
6 hard-boiled eggs, sliced
5 small potatoes, cooked, peeled, and sliced
Fresh parsley sprigs, celery sticks, and green onions,
if desired, for garnish

Cook and drain the bacon, crumble it and set it aside. Pour off all the drippings but 1 teaspoon; into that teaspoonful, blend the flour, sugar, salt, fresh pepper, if desired, celery seeds, dry mustard, and garlic. Simmer this over low heat until it is smooth. Add the combined water and vinegar to the sauce, stirring and simmering until it is again smooth and begins to thicken. Reserve 2 of the egg slices for garnish; chop the remaining slices and add to the sauce with the potato slices and reserved bacon. Gently stir the salad and heat it to serving temperature, allowing the sauce to thicken. Serve it garnished with the reserved egg slices and, if desired, with parsley, celery, and green onions. SERVES 4.

Maye's Oyster House
A Favorite of "Jimmy the Good"

Since 1867, Maye's Oyster House has catered to the great and near-great from all corners of the world. It was our beloved governor, "Jimmy the Good" Rolph, who had his own special corner and favorite dishes at this venerable restaurant. One would like to think that other California governors with Rolph's good taste had followed suit. A recipe for old-time, country-style minestrone as it was served eighty years ago, has survived with the generally preferred long-cooking method.

SAN FRANCISCO OLD-TIME MINESTRONE

4 vegetables of the season, sliced
4 tablespoons bacon drippings
1½ teaspoons salt
Coarsely ground black pepper to taste
2 tablespoons flour
5 cups beef stock
1 cup dry red wine
¼ cup diced salt pork
2 bay leaves
3 cloves garlic, chopped
2 teaspoons celery seeds
1 potato, peeled and sliced
6 medium tomatoes, sliced
½ cup kidney beans, cooked
½ cup garbanzo beans, cooked
1 cup small imported pasta
Spices and other additions, as desired

In a large pot, braise the seasonal vegetables to be used (such as zucchini, squash, and carrots) in the drippings. Add salt and pepper
and enough flour to thicken the mixture slightly, and stir it well.
Add the soup stock, red wine, pork, bay leaves, garlic and celery
seeds. Simmer these ingredients for about 2 hours over a very low
heat. Add potato, tomatoes, and beans. When the potato is almost
tender, add the small pasta; cook the soup until the pasta is tender.
Remove the bay leaves before serving the minestrone. This soup ages
very well, and it tastes richer when rewarmed. Other spices and ingredients can be added or substituted to the cook's taste, and, in fact,
such adaptations are traditional. Nothing substitutes for homemade
beef stock, of course, but canned stock may be used when time is
essential. SERVES 6 TO 8.

MAYE'S OYSTER HOUSE, a Polk Street landmark since 1867
Photo courtesy of the San Francisco Archives, San Francisco Public Library

Bohemian Caesar's
Where They Sang "Down Went McGinty"

Caesar's Bohemian Restaurant sat at the heart of the Latin Quarter, near the notorious old Barbary Coast. Like other eateries in the area, Caesar's was famous for hearty but cheap *table d'hôte* fare. Here are some examples of what was offered:

The Four-Bits (50¢) Dinner: Four different hors d'oeuvres, five salads, two soups, several different fish dishes, assorted pasta, chicken, ice cream or a rum omelet, mixed fresh fruit, and coffee.
The Dollar Dinner: Salami and anchovies, green salad, minestrone, fillet of sole, pasta, veal scallopini with caper sauce, vegetables, roast chicken, ice cream or fried cream, pastries, and coffee.
The Twelve-Bits ($1.50) Dinner: Salami and anchovies, green salad with assorted vegetables, a fancy pasta, minestrone, salmon or bass, ravioli with mushrooms, chicken, a small squab, zabaglione, fresh fruits and cheeses, and coffee.

The grandest, most expensive dinner in these Bohemian restaurants rarely exceeded $3.50 per person. Even so, the highest-priced meal was considered the choice of spendthrifts and high rollers. A small carafe of good table wine was served with the four-bits dinner at no extra charge. "The Dead-Slow Set" and the conservatives in the city considered Bohemia's cafés to be social evils, but nobody could suppress the customers' lust for good food, laughter, dancing, and the singing of "Down Went McGinty" with variable risqué poesy.

Caesar's, and any other North Beach restaurant worth its salt, either made pasta every day, or bought it freshly produced in the quarter. It emerged from the virgin dough as a variety of toothsome pasta delicacies from *tortellini* to *fettuccine*. This recipe for North Beach pasta is in the tradition of northern Italy, where oil, water, and salt are deliberately omitted. Approximately ten servings.

NORTH BEACH EGG PASTA

6 eggs
6 cups flour

Here is the way to make excellent homemade pasta. Combine the eggs and flour, but take care that the dough does not become too dry. Exact proportions will vary according to the ingredients and the weather, but as a rule, not more than one cup of flour to one egg. The blend should be well mixed and rather crumbly. Next, knead the dough to a smooth consistency. This should be done with your hands and it should take approximately ten minutes. Separate the pasta into three balls and roll out, or roll out the entire batch. The dough should be flattened into a width of one-fourth inch. If the mixture is sticky, dust it with flour as you work the roller. To finish the procedure, once again roll the dough, this time until it is so thin as to be virtually transparent. The pasta will wrap itself around the roller, and it should be pulled sideways as many times as it takes to reach the desired consistency. Do not take longer than ten minutes to finish rolling and forming. For stuffing, do not allow the pasta to dry; keep the surface moist at all times. Form and fill the dough as soon as it is ready, each pasta according to its own recipe. This mixture may be put through any of the excellent automatic machines, or, after drying from twenty to thirty minutes, cut by hand. YIELDS ABOUT 1½ POUNDS.

San Francisco is known the world over for its superb Italian cuisine, whether Genovese, Romano, Bolognese, or di Napoli. Equally spectacular are the various pastries and desserts created in these regions, all of which are faithfully and lovingly duplicated in San Francisco's fine Italian restaurants.

OLD-TIME SAN FRANCISCO SPONGE CAKE

1 teaspoon vanilla
1 teaspoon grated orange peel
½ cup water
1 cup sugar
6 eggs, separated

1 cup sifted cake flour
½ teaspoon salt
½ teaspoon cream of tartar

Preheat oven to 350 degrees F. Have all the ingredients ready at room temperature. Combine the vanilla, orange peel, water, and sugar in a bowl and mix them well. Beat in the egg yolks with a mixer or vigorously with a whisk until the mixture is light in color, thick and fluffy. Fold in the flour. Add the salt to the egg whites and beat them until foamy; sprinkle the cream of tartar over the egg whites and continue to beat them until they are stiff but not dry. Fold the flour-egg mixture into the egg whites. Turn the batter into an ungreased 10 × 4-inch tube pan. Bake the cake for about 50 minutes; it should spring back when lightly touched with a fork or finger. Invert the pan on a cake rack and cool it completely before loosening the sides with a knife and turning it out. SERVES 6 TO 8.

SICILIAN RUM CAKE

1 sponge cake
6 tablespoons rum
1 recipe Classic Zabaglione
1 cup whipped cream

Split the sponge cake into 4 layers and sprinkle them with at least 6 tablespoons of rum. Fill the layers with cool zabaglione. Refrigerate the cake, and just before serving it, frost it with whipped cream lightly flavored with rum. SERVES 6.

CLASSIC ZABAGLIONE

6 egg yolks
6 tablespoons granulated sugar
Pinch of salt
6 tablespoons sweet sherry

Combine the egg yolks, sugar, and salt in the upper part of a cold double boiler. Beat the mixture with a rotary beater until thick and lemon-colored. Gradually beat in the sweet sherry. Place mixture over hot but not boiling water and beat again until thick and fluffy like whipped cream. Remove from the heat and spoon the dessert into champagne or sherbert glasses. Either serve warm or very, very cold. SERVES 4 TO 6.

The most luxurious, expensive, and cherished Italian dessert served in San Francisco is *Zuppa Inglese*, and it has held this premier position since the Gaslight Era.

ZUPPA INGLESE

3 egg yolks
2 cups milk
¼ cup sugar
¼ cup flour
1 tablespoon grated lemon peel
1 tablespoon grated orange peel
1 (10-inch) layer sponge cake
1 cup Triple Sec
½ cup raspberry jam
½ pint heavy cream
Sugar to taste
Sliced almonds, to cook's touch
Other fresh or glacé fruit, if desired

Beat the egg yolks slightly, and then carefully beat in the milk, sugar, and flour. Strain this through a fine sieve into a saucepan. Add the lemon and orange peel. Cook the mixture over a low heat, stirring constantly until it comes to a boil. Then immediately remove the custard from the heat and cool the pan quickly in a basin of cold water. Bring the custard to room temperature. Cut the sponge cake crosswise, into 3 layers. Center the bottom layer on a cake plate and sprinkle it with ½ amount of Triple Sec. When the liqueur is absorbed, spread the cake with half the jam and half the custard. Top this with the middle layer. Again, sprinkle the remaining Triple Sec on the cake and let it be absorbed, then spread on the remaining jam and custard. Whip the cream, beat in sugar to taste, and frost the cake with whipped cream. Garnish it with almonds. Strawberries or other fresh fruit or glacé fruits may also be used as garnishes. SERVES 6 TO 8.

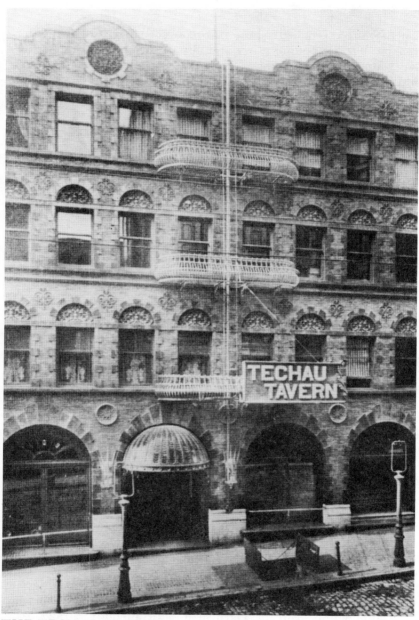

THE TECHAU TAVERN
Photo courtesy of the San Francisco Archives, San Francisco Public Library

The Techau Tavern
The Good-Time Place

The old Techau Tavern reverberated with wild music and loud singing of rough songs, but the food was both refined and admirable. A
fragile, little booklet issued by the Sperry Products people at the
century's turn contains Chef Charles Strandberg's recipe for an authentic Austrian torte and mocha filling:

THE TECHAU TORTE

    6 eggs
    4 ounces sugar
    4 ounces flour
    4 ounces melted butter
    Mocha Torte Filling

Preheat oven to 350 degrees F. Beat the eggs and sugar in a bowl
over a pot of hot water or in a double boiler until warm. Then remove
the bowl from the hot water and beat the eggs and sugar until they
are cold and very light. Add the flour, mix the batter until it is light,
and add the butter, once more mixing until light. Bake the batter
in a greased round baking pan about 10 inches across for 25 minutes.
When cake is cool, remove from pan and cut into 3 layers. Between
them, spread the Mocha Torte Filling. SERVES 6 TO 8.

MOCHA TORTE FILLING

    6 ounces sweet butter
    4 egg whites
    5 ounces sugar
    ¼ cup water
    Coffee extract, to cook's touch

Work the sweet butter until it is creamy. Beat the egg whites to a stiff froth. In a saucepan, dissolve the sugar in the ¼ cup water and boil it until the syrup forms a soft ball when dropped into cold water. Pour the cooked sugar into the stiff egg whites, stirring them together. When the sugar-egg white mixture has cooled, stir in the butter and coffee extract. Spread it generously between torte layers. Yields enough for a 10-inch layer cake.

Luna's on Vallejo
Part Old Mexican, Part Early Californian

Luna's, the city's first notable Mexican restaurant, was located at the corner of Vallejo and Grant at the edge of the "Mexican" slope of Telegraph Hill. Neither fancy nor expensive, the restaurant was friendly, cozy, and frequented by a loyal clientele. *Capirotada*, an old-fashioned Mexican pudding, was one of the chef's most popular desserts.

TELEGRAPH HILL *CAPIROTADA*

1 cup sugar
2 cups water
1 teaspoon cinnamon
Dash of nutmeg
½ teaspoon salt
6 slices of bread, toasted
1½ cups shredded Cheddar cheese
½ cup raisins
½ cup seedless dates
¼ cup salted peanuts
2 tablespoons butter

Preheat oven to 350 degrees F. In a saucepan over medium heat, cook the sugar, stirring constantly, until it melts and becomes amber-colored. Remove the pan from the heat and stir in the water, cinnamon, nutmeg, and salt. Cook this mixture over low heat, again stirring constantly, until the caramel has dissolved and the mixture is well blended. Remove it from the heat. Then arrange a layer of torn-up toasted bread in a greased 2-quart casserole, and sprinkle it with some of the cheese, raisins, dates, and peanuts. Repeat these layers until all the bread, cheese, raisins, dates, and peanuts are used. Dot the top of the pudding with the butter, and then pour the syrup over the mixture. Bake it until the syrup is absorbed—as much as 30 minutes. SERVES 4 TO 6 AS A DESSERT.

Variations of *Capirotada* include the addition of small chunks of apple, or of a little aniseed in the syrup, the substitution of piñones or pine nuts for the peanuts, and a garnish of kiwi slices.

Another Luna favorite was a dessert named Sweet Tamale, a concoction of egg yolks, cinnamon, raisins, and nuts enclosed in a light crust and baked until nut brown. It was much like *Capirotada*.

Tait-Zinkand's
Hearty Fare with a German Accent

The Tait-Zinkand's Restaurant at 168 O'Farrell was a combination of two great San Francisco establishments. Although the restaurant offered an enormous international menu, it was particularly celebrated for superb German entrées. Georges Milhau, who became the chef of the merged houses, had a great sense of humor. The jolly cook preserved Frederick the Great's favorite dish for posterity by serving a simplified, practical version of the famous beef entrée. It was passed along to him via the culinary network. Ernest Otzenberger, who cooked for the George Whitney Vanderbilts, brought the recipe to America. He gave it to Chef Fischel, the pupil of the famous Jean Marie Laporte, when they were both in New York City. Fischel taught Emile Bailly how to make the dish, and the latter brought it to San Francisco and served it at the Fairmont. Milhau, who was Bailly's assistant for a time, then took the recipe to Tait-Zinkand's. The German monarch, as triumphant at the dinner table as he was victorious in battle, would have agreed that his adored dish traveled well! The entrée amused Milhau as he thought of it as a *folie de grandeur*.

FREDERICK THE GREAT'S BEEF TENDERLOIN

          1 (3-pound) cut of beef tenderloin
          Salt and pepper to taste
          4 tablespoons olive oil
          2 large pieces of thinly sliced veal
          1 tablespoon butter
          1 onion, finely chopped
          1 clove garlic
          2 shallots, finely chopped
          1 teaspoon flour
          2 cups brown gravy

TAIT-ZINKAND'S CAFÉ
Photo courtesy of the San Francisco Archives, San Francisco Public Library

½ cup tomato sauce
½ cup white wine
12 whole mushrooms
8 small, browned, cooked and peeled potatoes
Fresh parsley sprigs, to cook's touch
Radishes, to cook's touch

Preheat oven to 350 degrees F. Season the cut of beef with salt and pepper, and sauté the meat on each side in olive oil. Remove the meat from the pan, reserving the pan with the drippings, and cover the tenderloin with the pieces of veal, tying them on securely. Return the meat to the reserved pan and sauté the meat for 5 more minutes in the drippings, this time adding the butter and chopped onion, the garlic clove, and the shallots. Then stir in well the teaspoon of flour. Moisten these ingredients with the brown gravy, tomato sauce, and white wine, and add the mushrooms. Bake the whole for 20 minutes with the browned potatoes. Serve the tenderloin sliced, garnished with the fresh parsley and radishes. SERVES 6 TO 8 AS AN ENTRÉE.

Milhau had a favorite recipe for Russian borscht that he insisted on keeping as a staple on the menu at the Tait-Zinkand café. This old-fashioned recipe for the rich soup is one which Milhau preserved in *Recipes of the World-Famous Chefs*.

MILHAU'S OLD-FASHIONED RUSSIAN BORSCHT

1 duck, roasted to a light color
1 pound breast of beef, boiled and drained
¼ pound lean salt pork, boiled
1 beetroot (fresh beet), shredded, with its juice
1 leek, shredded
1 onion, shredded
½ head cabbage, shredded
Fresh parsley, chopped, to cook's touch
Celery, shredded, to cook's touch
2 tablespoons butter
3 cups consommé
Bag (cheesecloth) of fennel, marjoram, thyme, bay leaves, cloves
4 large French mushrooms (cèpes), or any large, fleshy mushroom
2 ounces nut sausage
2 teaspoons sour cream

Simmer down the vegetables in butter. Add the consommé, then add the duck, the breast of beef, the salt pork, the bag of herbs, and the mushrooms. Bring this to a boil and skim it well. Add the sausage. Simmer for 30 minutes. Then remove the meat and slice it. Remove the herb bag and skim off the grease. Add the sour cream, thinned with the beet juice, as needed. Serve the soup very hot, with the sliced meat on the side as garniture.

The Old Tivoli

An Honored Member of the Family

The name Tivoli has always been featured in San Francisco, whether attached to a theater, hotel, opera house, or restaurant. And equally venerable in San Francisco is the custom of sopping robust foods and sauces with chunks of homemade bread and biscuits. The Old Tivoli was known to serve a variety of such breads, and though the restaurant's own formulations have not been handed down, these rich recipes are typical of the era.

FRESH CORN FRITTERS

6 medium ears fresh corn, uncooked
¼ cup sifted flour
2 tablespoons sugar
¼ teaspoon salt
¼ teaspoon white pepper
1 egg, beaten
2 tablespoons shredded sharp Cheddar cheese
1 cup pure vegetable oil

Remove the corn kernels from cobs, and mix with flour, sugar, salt, and white pepper. Then blend in the beaten egg and Cheddar cheese. In a deep frying pan, add cooking oil to depth of at least 2 inches and heat to 375 degrees F. Drop teaspoonfuls of mixture into oil and cook until they are golden brown. Drain the fritters and serve immediately. SERVES 6 TO 8 AS AN APPETIZER.

TABLE D'HÔTE BISCUITS

2 cups all-purpose flour
1 tablespoon baking powder
1 teaspoon salt
1 cup cold sweet butter
2 eggs, beaten
½ cup heavy cream

Preheat oven to 450 degrees F. Sift the flour, and sift it again with the baking powder and salt. Cut the cold butter into the flour mix until its texture becomes coarse but somewhat even—leave in the smaller lumps. Form a well in the center of the flour mixture, and pour in the beaten eggs together with the heavy cream. Lightly mix but do not work the dough, which will be very soft. Roll out the dough on a lightly floured bread board to a thickness of ½ inch. Form it again into a ball and roll it out twice more. Then cut the dough into 2-inch rounds and bake them on an ungreased cookie sheet for about 15 minutes, or until they are puffed and golden brown on top. Serve immediately. YIELDS 10 TO 12 BISCUITS.

POLK GULCH CINNAMON ROLLS

2 cups biscuit dough
3 tablespoons soft butter
½ cup loosely packed brown sugar
3 teaspoons cinnamon
½ teaspoon nutmeg

Preheat oven to 450 degrees F. Roll out the biscuit dough on a floured surface to a ¼-inch thickness. Spread it with soft butter and pat the sugar, cinnamon, and nutmeg over it. Roll up the dough like a jelly roll, and cut it in 1-inch-thick slices. Bake them in a well-greased pan for about 15 minutes. YIELDS 10 TO 12 ROLLS.

THE OLD TIVOLI CAFÉ on Eddy Street, in 1905
Photo courtesy of the San Francisco Archives, San Francisco Public Library

Bernstein's Fish Grotto
The Pride of Powell Street

Bernstein's, until recently a Powell Street landmark, opened its doors for the first time soon after the earthquake. From its inception the restaurant kept cioppino, the famous San Francisco fish stew, on the menu. Early in this century, more than one hundred and nine varieties of fish were taken from San Francisco Bay and sold commercially by the fishermen who hailed mainly from Genoa. In those golden days, our bay was as bountiful as their own Ligurian Sea. A great treat rarely savored today is cioppino cooked on the small boats while at sea, with the catch prepared immediately after having been scooped from the cold waters. In that more leisurely era, this was a feast that was regularly enjoyed. Cioppino remains on the menus of most of the city's fine fish restaurants, and its variety of ingredients is infinite. Our recipe for the succulent stew is the one that is basic to San Francisco, but the inventive cook can readily add or subtract items to enhance its aroma and taste.

GOLDEN GATE SELECT CIOPPINO

¼ cup butter
1 onion, sliced
¼ cup olive oil
1 clove garlic, crushed
6 fresh tomatoes
24 small, fresh mushrooms
1 (6-ounce) can tomato paste
2 teaspoons dried basil
1 teaspoon dried oregano
2 teaspoons celery salt
1 teaspoon celery seeds
½ cup fresh lemon juice

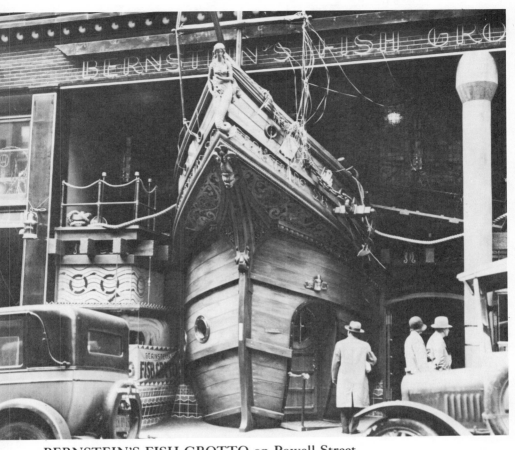

BERNSTEIN'S FISH GROTTO on Powell Street
Photo courtesy of the San Francisco Archives, San Francisco Public Library

1½ cups dry red wine
½ cup garlic-flavored red wine vinegar
¼ cup dry vermouth
Tomato sauce or red wine vinegar to thin cioppino,
    if necessary
1½ pounds cook's choice of fish, cleaned, in chunks
1½ pounds cook's choice of shellfish, cleaned and shelled
½ pound fresh shelled crab meat
12 clams in their shells, if desired

In a heavy, large pot, melt the butter and sauté the onion until it is golden. Add the olive oil and lightly sauté the garlic, fresh tomatoes, and mushrooms. Then add the tomato paste, basil, oregano, celery salt, celery seeds, lemon juice, red wine, red wine vinegar, and vermouth. Bring these to a quick boil and simmer for 1 hour, stirring occasionally. Thin this sauce with tomato sauce or more red wine, if necessary. When sauce has cooked, add the fresh fish, shellfish, and crab and simmer them for 20 minutes. Add the clams and cook cioppino for an additional 10 minutes, or until the shells open. SERVES 6 TO 8.

The key to this recipe is to experiment! Leave something out— substitute something else. The cook can be wonderfully creative with this dish. Serve the cioppino with generous helpings of San Francisco's unique sourdough French bread—and a very large bib!

St. Germain

The Glory of the Eye and the Palate

Originally founded in 1895, St. Germain was noted for its cosmopolitan menu and its colorful, eye-pleasing locale. One St. Germain specialty that has survived the test of time is *Fritto Misto*, which means literally "fried mixture." This mélange included almost any vegetables in season, small pieces of raw shrimp or crab meat, Italian squash, asparagus, cauliflower, and also lamb or veal, in small pieces, or sweetbreads. Small onions, green beans, and broccoli were usually part of the selection.

BATTER FOR SAN FRANCISCO *FRITTO MISTO*

2 cups flour
Salt to taste
¼ teaspoon black pepper
4 eggs, separated
12 ounces beer
3 dashes of Tabasco sauce
½ cup melted butter
Oil
Desired vegetables and meats, cut into small pieces
Fresh lime juice

Mix the flour, a little salt, and the pepper. Beat the egg yolks and combine them with flour and seasonings; add the beer and stir the batter until it is blended. Add several dashes of Tabasco. Stir in the melted butter, and let the batter stand at room temperature for 1½ hours. Then beat the egg whites until stiff, and fold them into the batter. Heat the oil of your choice to 400 degrees F. Dip pieces of raw vegetables and meats into the batter, sprinkle them with lime juice, and deep-fry them individually until they are golden brown.
SERVES 4 TO 6 AS AN APPETIZER.

ST. GERMAIN RESTAURANT
Photo courtesy of the San Francisco Archives, San Francisco Public Library

DELMONICO'S and its staff
Photo courtesy of the California Historical Society, San Francisco

Delmonico's

Fit for Kings of the Day and Queens of the Night

Situated on O'Farrell Street for several decades, Delmonico's was one of the five great restaurants in San Francisco catering to the best French tradition. The food was supreme, the furnishings were gorgeous, the crystal was imported, and the ambiance was superb. Unfortunately, the restaurant burned to the ground in the Great Fire of 1906. In remembrance of Delmonico's, and of that more than spectacular conflagration, here is a recipe for Fried Cream, a dessert whose local popularity continues to this day. It demands a great fire of its own!

FRIED CREAM

1 pint heavy cream
3 teaspoons white rum, plus additional, for flambéeing
¼ teaspoon salt
½ cup sugar
1 stick of cinnamon
3 tablespoons cornstarch
3 tablespoons milk
3 egg yolks
⅓ cup finely grated almonds
1 egg, beaten
⅓ cup saltine cracker crumbs
Oil

In a small saucepan, scald the heavy cream. Add the rum, salt, sugar, cinnamon stick, and the cornstarch. Dissolve ingredients in the milk. Simmer this mixture long enough to remove the starchy taste, then add the egg yolks and transfer the cream to the top of a double boiler. Over boiling water, cook it, stirring constantly, until it is thick. Remove the cinnamon stick, and pour the cream into a flat dish to a depth of about ¾ inch. When the cream is cool and firm, turn over the dish and slide the cream out on a flat board; cut the cream into oblongs, and roll in the finely grated almonds. Then dip each oblong in the beaten whole egg and roll it gently in cracker crumbs. Chill the cream. When it is firm, fry the oblongs quickly in oil heated to 400 degrees F. just long enough to turn the almonds golden. Pour additional white rum over the fried cream, carefully set it afire, and serve the dessert flaming. SERVES 4.

GIRARD'S FRENCH RESTAURANT
Photo courtesy of the San Francisco Archives, San Francisco Public Library

Girard's

Where They Did It Best in French

Girard's French Restaurant, once operating at 65 Ellis Street, was owned by a French-Canadian, Wilfred J. Girard. In 1890, the proprietor moved the operation to new quarters where more than six hundred people could be served in any given day. Girard's was justly famous for its exclusive version of French dressing, which was bottled for public sale in the 1930s. It is still sold under the same name, although not precisely in the original formula.

CLASSIC SAN FRANCISCO FRENCH DRESSING

1 egg, beaten
2 teaspoons Dijon mustard or ½ teaspoon dry mustard
½ cup white vinegar
2 tablespoons imported olive oil
¼ cup water
1 tablespoon finely ground bread crumbs
¼ teaspoon chopped fresh garlic
Salt to taste
1½ teaspoons sugar
¼ teaspoon white pepper

Combine all ingredients in an electric blender and process for about 30 seconds. Refrigerate the dressing, and serve it cold. The flavor of the dressing is improved when it is refrigerated overnight. This recipe has a touch of garlic—but then it would not be San Franciscan without it! YIELDS ENOUGH FOR 2 DINNER SALADS.

Jack's
The Greatest Survivor

San Francisco has no greater culinary achievement than the venerable Jack's Restaurant. Functioning superbly since 1864, it has been directed by the Redinger family since the turn of the century. Through the courtesy of Mr. J. P. Redinger, we present Jack's famous recipe for Sole Marguery, as it is still delightfully served today.

JACK'S FILLET OF SOLE MARGUERY

½ cup butter
3 pounds fillet of sole
1 cup sliced mushrooms
12 medium Alaska king crab legs, shelled
1 cup tiny bay shrimps
Shallots, chopped fine, to cook's touch
1 cup dry white wine
½ cup fish stock or water
Salt and ground pepper to taste
½ cup heavy cream
3 tablespoons hollandaise sauce

Preheat oven to 350 degrees F. Spread some of the butter around a baking dish that can also be used over direct heat. Arrange in it the fillets, sliced mushrooms, meat from the crab legs, shrimps, chopped shallots, white wine, stock or water, and the salt and pepper. Dot the top with the remaining butter. Bake the fish for 15 minutes. When cooked, remove all ingredients except the liquid to a heatproof platter. To the liquid remaining in the baking dish, add the heavy cream, and over low heat, reduce it to a thick sauce. Remove from heat and then add the hollandaise—mix it well, but do not cook the sauce again. Pour it over the sole, and lightly glaze the fish under preheated broiler for a few seconds. SERVES 4 TO 6 AS AN ENTRÉE.

Hang Far Low
Chinatown, a Jade Kingdom by the Bay

San Francisco's Chinatown was the most thriving oriental community outside China from the middle of the nineteenth century well into the twentieth. At one time, during those highbinding decades, more than thirty thousand Chinese were crowded into its murky corridors. Today's Chinatown, still a center for arriving Asians, is now greatly reserved—in comparison with the times when *boo hoy doy*, hired assassins, roamed dark alleys. But Chinatown's exotic fare, mysterious stairs leading to underground parlors, and private clubs barred with double doors seemed always to fascinate and beckon the most casual visitor to San Francisco, in spite of the many dangers.

Openly for hire in Chinatown, as elsewhere in the city, were the sensuous vices. According to reports in *The Annals of San Francisco*, two Chinese courtesans, Ah Toy and Selina, were the favorites of the area. Ah Toy operated in the 1850s, becoming a wealthy madame and retiring to China with her substantial profits. Selina acquired her fame in the late 1880s with an innovative gimmick: She would charge fifty cents for a "lookie" at her beautiful nude body; more overt favors would cost the customer one full dollar.

The wonderful names of Chinatown's original restaurants have generally vanished. It's a pity that the Chamber of Tranquility, Gardens of Plants of Jade, and the Chamber of Celestial Odors no longer exist. After the devastation of 1906, the Hang Far Low Palace at 723 Grant Avenue became the best-known restaurant of the quarter. It was recognized as the symbol of all that was superb and adventurous in Chinese cuisine. Regretfully, its lyrical Chinese name became the butt of many rude jokes by low-minded, English-speaking San Franciscans. . . .

Chop suey and chow mein are rightfully considered little more than Americanized garbage by oriental gourmets. Both of these ersatz recipes are about as Chinese as *tacos!* Some scholars insist that chop suey was invented in San Francisco in the 1890s by an unknown Chinese on Dupont Street. Herbert Asbury, in his *Barbary Coast*, suggests that it was an original contribution to a banquet in New York given by Li Hung Chang, a Mandarin statesman. Supposedly, the diplomat's chef was ordered to create one dish the Occidental guests would be sure to enjoy. The resourceful chef prepared a stew flavored with soy sauce, which he named "chop suey," literally meaning "odds and ends." Remarkably, the mongrel recipe gained universal popularity and now is a staple of the American diet.

One of the most curious turn-of-the-century Chinese recipes we have discovered probably cannot be duplicated today. Nevertheless, it is so exquisite and individual that we have included it here in its precious entirety. Perhaps one of the thousand delights of original Cantonese cuisine at its zenith, this recipe from the Hang Far Low restaurant must have been intended for the *adventurous*—and not for the overly squeamish—initiate.

REED BIRDS *À LA CHINOISE*

Purchase 2 or 3 cans of Chinese reed birds from a shop in the Grant Avenue district. Take the birds out of their containers. In a large, greased pan, heat the birds thoroughly. Toast old-fashioned digestive crackers and on each one place 2 of the reed birds. Serve them on very hot plates. Accompany this dish with a sparkling white wine of golden hue.

This dish was also a standard at Hang Far Low:

ROSS VALLEY *CHAR SIEW*

    1 pound pork tenderloin, cut into strips
    ¼ cup sugar
    ½ cup honey
    ½ cup soy sauce
    1 teaspoon garlic powder
    ½ teaspoon powdered hot (English) mustard
    ½ teaspoon salt
    3 tablespoons chili sauce
    Sesame seeds, to cook's touch, for garnish
    Oil

UNIDENTIFIED CHINATOWN RESTAURANT A typical
example in the 800 block of Jackson Street before the Great Earthquake
Photo courtesy of the California Section, California State Library

Marinate the pork in a combination of the sugar, honey, soy sauce, garlic powder, hot mustard, salt, and chili sauce for at least 3 hours. If possible, prepare the dish ahead to this stage and marinate the pork overnight in the refrigerator. Turn the meat from time to time. When ready to cook, preheat the broiler to 425 degrees F. Drain the pork and broil it for no less than 20 minutes. Turn the strips every 5 minutes. While they are cooking, toast the sesame seeds by heating them until golden in a pan with just enough oil to coat them. When the pork strips are cooked through and browned, arrange them on a hot platter. Sprinkle the barbecue pork with toasted sesame seeds, and serve the pork immediately. SERVES 4 AS AN APPETIZER.

V.

HOWEVER, NOT ALL THE GREAT COOKS WERE MEN

THE SUPERB CULINARY ACCOMPLISHMENTS OF SAN FRANCISCO'S WOMAN-kind were rarely allowed public exposure in the early days of the city's gastronomical growth, of course; instead, "decent" women were expected to practice their arts, culinary or otherwise, within the sanctified confines of hearth and home. However, the preciously held taboo used against women to deny them the high status of "establishment" chefs—a prejudice rooted in European culture that was later promulgated coast-to-coast in our own country until wisely put to death in recent modern times—ironically afforded the city's "gentler" sex a unique opportunity to excel on three parallel, equally important culinary levels: they compiled invaluable anthologies of historic food preparations; they conserved marvelous chronicles of indispensable home cures and herbal practices; as hostesses, they set a precedent of unmatched charm and brilliance that has been exquisitely preserved by the city's subsequent generation of women.

Those women of an earlier San Francisco sprang from divergent heritages. Luckily for us who treasure their recipes, they left us many records of multiethnic cookery and—whether "pure" Yankee, Hispanic, or everything-else-in-between—their recipes helped in no small way to establish the variant, always fascinating character of today's California cuisine.

The Brigade of Yankee Women

After the Gold Rush, an ever-growing number of resolute, no-nonsense Yankee women arrived in San Francisco to set up housekeeping. They brought with them their own strict traditions and rather rigid mores. Most of them were exceedingly thrifty. In a little booklet entitled *The California Recipe Book*, published in 1872 in San Francisco, we found the following recipes, which were set forth by "The Ladies of California," anonymous San Franciscans, all! (Wherever possible, the recipes are presented as they appear in the booklet, without modern additions, because of historic appeal.)

HOMEMADE TOMATO CATSUP
by
"A Lady of Mason Street"

2 gallons tomatoes
1 quart cider vinegar
7 tablespoons salt
2½ tablespoons black pepper
1½ tablespoons cayenne pepper
1½ tablespoons allspice
1 tablespoon whole cloves
3 heaping tablespoons dry mustard

Skin the tomatoes, boil and strain them. Combine the other ingredients with the tomatoes and cook over a slow heat for 4 hours. Cool slightly, place in jars, and cover tightly to store.

PRESERVED GREEN TOMATOES
by
"A Lady of Laguna Street"

> 1 peck (8 quarts) green tomatoes
> 1 cup salt
> 2 cups granulated sugar
> 2 tablespoons whole cloves
> 2 tablespoons allspice
> 2 tablespoons cinnamon
> 8 green peppers, finely chopped
> 24 onions, chopped
> 1 quart chopped cabbage
> Cider vinegar (to cover)

Slice the tomatoes and sprinkle with salt. Let stand overnight. Drain off the liquid, add the sugar, cloves, allspice, cinnamon, peppers, onions, and cabbage. Cover the ingredients with cider vinegar and boil vigorously for 15 minutes. Cool slightly, place in jars, and cover tightly to store.

"The Ladies of California" also much favored candied rose and violet petals. In the late nineteenth century, they had ample leisure to undertake the preparation of this unusual delicacy. Their archaic but utterly charming recipe for Candied Rose Leaves is presented *exactly* as they wrote it over a century ago:

"THE LADIES" CANDIED ROSE LEAVES

Select the desired quantity of perfect rose leaves, spread them on an inverted sieve, and let them stand in the air until slightly dried but not crisp. Make a syrup from a half-pound granulated sugar and a half-pint of water, and boil the mixture until it spins a thread; then lift the leaves in and out of the hot syrup using a fine wire sieve. Then let the leaves stand for several hours on a slightly oiled surface (or waxed paper). If the rose leaves then look preserved and clean, they will not require a second dipping. Then melt a cup of fondant (use a basic vanilla icing), and add 2 drops of essence of rose and 2 drops of cochineal (herbal rose food coloring) to the melted icing. Then dip the rose leaves into the mixture one at a time. Dust with fine confectioner's or powdered sugar and place on oiled (or waxed) paper to harden. (Then pick *daintily*, and enjoy as you would candy drops!)

While undertaking the laborious process of creating Candied Rose Leaves, "The Ladies" often indulged themselves with a bite or two of their circle's Tipsey Cake—no doubt a soothing reward for their errant husbands' habitual tramping along the Cocktail Route.

SAN FRANCISCO TIPSEY CAKE

Cut 1 loaf of pound cake in half and place each half in a glass casserole. Liberally sprinkle the cake with blanched raisins. Wet the cake plentifully with a fine sherry, dropping raspberry jelly on top, and have ready a nice custard sauce also liberally laced with sherry to pour over the cake. (*Voilà!* Tipsey Cake!)

Crumbs and Common Sense

As time went by, women culinary chroniclers began to shed their anonymity. In 1902, a slim volume appeared under the title *Crumbs from Everybody's Table*, proudly edited by Mrs. R. L. Porter of the Monterey Peninsula. Although not a San Francisco resident, Mrs. Porter must have been quite a city-sophisticate because the chef of San Francisco's opulent Occidental Hotel (alas, that beautiful edifice fell victim to the 1906 fire) gallantly allowed the lady to use his prized oyster recipe in her cookbook. (The recipe appears as printed in the original volume.)

ANGELS ON HORSEBACK

Lemon juice
Cayenne pepper
Anchovy paste
Oysters
Bacon
Butter
Toast, buttered

Mix in a saucer fresh lemon juice and cayenne pepper (to the cook's taste). Add some anchovy paste and blend the ingredients well. Dip the [shelled] oysters in the mixture, and then wrap them in bacon [strips]. Melt the butter in a skillet and fry the appetizers until the bacon is done [crisp]. Serve on buttered toast. Adjust quantities to the occasion at hand.

Since fresh vegetables were so readily available, chow chow—a nearly forgotten dish—was part of every Californian's cooking repertoire. The cook was expected to make it from scratch, concocting his or her own special variation of the basic recipe. Mrs. Porter offers at least a half-dozen chow chows in her cookbook. We present an all-purpose style.

CARMEL CHOW CHOW

18 medium cucumbers
2 large heads of cabbage
3 dozen small onions
18 green bell peppers
Salt, to cook's taste
2 tablespoons white mustard seeds
1 tablespoon celery seeds
2 (18-ounce) jars of dry mustard
1 pound sugar
1 quart cider vinegar, or more

Wash and slice the cucumbers without paring. Wash and chop the cabbage into fine pieces. Wash onions and remove the outer skins. Wash and dice the bell peppers and remove seeds. Mix the vegetables together in a suitable bowl, salt well, and let stand from 12 to 14 hours. Press the vegetables dry and place the mixture in a large saucepan or clay pot. Add the seasonings and mix very well. Cover the mixture with the cider vinegar. Use as much vinegar as necessary. Keep at a steady boil until mixture thickens. Cool and store. Reheat as needed to serve.

The following are two basic, no-nonsense-but-oh!-so-necessary entries from Mrs. Porter's cookbook:

PLAIN CHICKEN BROTH

1 fat stewing chicken
1 quart water
Salt, to cook's taste
1 carrot, peeled
½ cup diced celery

Cut the chicken into 4 parts, wash well in cold water, and place pieces in saucepan with the quart of water and salt. Bring mixture to boil, skim fat from top, and add the carrot and celery. Boil for additional 2 hours, then strain through a fine sieve.

BEEF TEA

1 quart cold water
1 pound lean round steak, diced
Salt, to cook's taste

Place the water in a double boiler and put the diced meat in upper part of pan. Add salt. Simmer the meat 3 to 4 hours. Then strain meat through a fine sieve, collecting the meat juice.

Mrs. Porter believed that some things were "well worth knowing" and she stated them plainly in her *Crumbs from Everybody's Table*. Surely the modern cook will agree that many of the following tips are *still* "well worth knowing."

THINGS WELL WORTH KNOWING

To keep celery two weeks, roll it in a brown bag, then in a towel, and store in a cool place. Before serving, place celery in a pan of ice-cold water for 1 hour.

To restore curdled mayonnaise, place a tablespoon of butter in a round-bottomed pan and gradually work in the mayonnaise.

To prevent cracking and chipping of new enameled cooking utensils, keep the insides greased with butter.

To clean bottles, decanters, and glass jugs, cut a lemon into small pieces, put into the glass containers with a little water, and shake vigorously. A slice of potato may be substituted for the lemon.

To prevent glass from breaking when pouring hot water into glassware, first put in a silver spoon or fork, and then pour the liquid. Allow the silver to remain in the glassware for a few minutes.

To ensure the best-textured baked potato, leave the skin on and cut off a small piece at the end before placing in the oven. When done, take the potato out with a cloth and press all sides well with hands.

To prevent scalded milk from curdling, add a pinch of soda before cooking.

To get rid of a fish bone stuck in the throat, immediately swallow a raw egg.

To remove wine stains, pour boiling water on the splotch before it has time to dry, then let it remain in boiling water for a few minutes.

To clean zinc, use a piece of soft flannel moistened with kerosene. To clean badly tarnished brass, rub it with salt and vinegar, or oxalic acid. Wash with soap and water and then polish brass vigorously.

To freshen the air in a room, place half an ounce of spirits of lavender and a lump of salt of ammonia in a wide-mouthed jar and leave uncovered.

To fix the colors in cotton goods, use salt. Dissolve a pint of salt in 4 gallons of water and soak the garments for an hour. The water must be kept cold.

A Classic from a Native Daughter

Señora Teresa Ynez Pinto, a daughter of the Old and New Worlds, practiced the best culinary traditions of both continents at her sprawling *estancia* in the nearby San Francisco countryside. A descendant of the grandees of Castile and the nobles of New Spain, she borrowed liberally from both cultures to blend a unique cuisine—Castiliano/Californiano. Shortly after the Great Earthquake and fire, she published some of her recipes in a delightful little volume, which has virtually vanished from sight, except for a treasured number preserved in a few private libraries. Her suggestion for a typical Spanish-American *cena*, or supper, is a super-classic:

CENA AT THE RANCHO

Caldillo de carne seca   (*dried beef soup*)
Chiles rellenos   (*stuffed peppers*)
Arroz gizado con tomate   (*fried rice with tomato*)
Pollo gizado   (*stewed-fried chicken*)
Macarrones con leche   (*macaroni with milk*)
Cajeta   (*quince candy*)

Pililas   (*sweet crisp wafers*)   Coffee and brandy

CALDILLO DE CARNE SECA

1 large round steak
Enough salt to dredge the steak
1 quart water
2 tablespoons butter
2 onions, chopped

1 tomato, diced
Sprinkle of freshly ground pepper, to cook's taste
3 eggs

Cut the steak into strips 1 inch wide. Dredge the strips with salt and hang to dry for seven or eight days. When meat is thoroughly dried, wash the salt from the strips and then boil them in a quart (or more) of water for 1 hour. Remove the meat (reserve the water) and let it cool a little. Then shred it with fingers. Melt the butter in a large frying pan, add the meat strips, onions, tomato, and ground pepper, and fry together for 15 minutes over low heat. Pour the reserved water over the mixture and allow to boil for 15 minutes. Just before serving, break 3 eggs into the soup and stir quickly. Serve soup very hot. SERVES 4 AMPLE PORTIONS OR 6 SMALLER PORTIONS.

CHILES RELLENOS

6 dried red chili peppers
4 tablespoons butter
2 onions, chopped
1 pound ground or finely diced beef
6 eggs

Take 6 dried red chili peppers and wash well. Cut off the tops and remove seeds and veins. Boil in a small amount of water until tender (15 or 20 minutes). While the peppers are cooking, take 2 tablespoons of butter, put in a skillet, and when melted, add the onions. Fry until golden. Add the beef to the skillet and cook until lightly browned. Remove the peppers from the water and drain. When peppers have cooled, stuff with meat mixture. In a separate bowl, beat eggs. Dip the stuffed peppers in the egg batter. Melt remaining butter in a skillet and then fry peppers until the egg coating is golden. Drain. Serve warm. SERVES 6.

ARROZ GIZADO CON TOMATE

2 tablespoons butter
1½ cups long-grain white rice

©1975 SPARE-TIME PRODUCTS, INC.

0011-8007

the GREAT GAME of

KISMET ®

SCORE SHEET

PLAYER'S NAME _____
(Each player keeps own score sheet)

BASIC SECTION	WHAT TO SCORE:	1st GAME	2nd GAME	3rd GAME	4th GAME	5th GAME	6th GAME
1. ACES	1 FOR EACH ACE	3	4	3	4	3	3
2. DEUCES	2 FOR EACH DEUCE	6	8	8	4	6	6
3. TREYS	3 FOR EACH TREY	12	12	12	9	9	12
4. FOURS	4 FOR EACH FOUR	16	16	11	12	8	4
5. FIVES	5 FOR EACH FIVE	15	15	15	15	20	20
6. SIXES	6 FOR EACH SIX		12	18	24	18	18
TOTAL		52	61	67	63	64	86
BONUS	IF 63-70 Score 35 ABOVE 71-77 Score 55 ▲ TOTAL IS 78 over Score 75				35	35	75
★ BASIC SECTION TOTAL ➡					100	99	161

1 onion, finely chopped
1 large tomato, diced
4 cups boiling water

Melt the butter in a deep skillet and pour rice into the pan. Add onions. Fry together until rice is light brown. Add the tomatoes. Sauté together. Then add 4 cups of boiling water, cover, and allow rice to simmer over low heat until rice is tender, about 20 minutes. More water may be added if needed. SERVES 4 GENEROUS PORTIONS.

POLLO GIZADO

1 large stewing chicken, disjointed
Salt to taste
Pepper to taste
Flour to coat chicken
3 tablespoons butter
1 onion, chopped

Wash chicken thoroughly and then place in large kettle with water. Boil until tender. Remove chicken and reserve 2 cups of the stock. Coat chicken pieces lightly with flour. Melt the butter in a large skillet, add the chicken, and sprinkle the onion around the chicken pieces. Fry until chicken is light brown. Then add the 2 cups of stock, salt and pepper, and allow chicken to simmer for 30 minutes. SERVES 4.

MACARRONES CON LECHE

1 pound macaroni (small, cut macaroni)
2 cups milk
½ cube butter

Preheat oven to 350 degrees F. Boil macaroni according to package directions until tender. Drain. Place macaroni in baking pan, and then pour the milk over the pasta. Dot the mixture with the butter. Place pan in oven and bake until the mixture is firm and the top is lightly browned. SERVES 4 TO 6.

CAJETA

2 dozen quinces, peeled and quartered
Sugar, as directed

Preheat oven to 350 degrees F. Wash the quartered quinces. Place quarters in boiling water and cook until thoroughly soft. Drain off the water and mash the quinces. For every cup of quince pulp add 1 cup of sugar. Stir well. Place mixture in deep-dish oven pan and bake for 20 minutes, or until mixture becomes completely dry. The compote should be glazed, clear, and transparent. Cool. Cut into small squares for serving.

PILILAS

2 cups flour
¼ teaspoon baking powder
Pinch of salt
1 tablespoon butter
¼ cup milk
2 cups hot, melted butter

Mix flour, baking powder, salt, butter, and milk and roll into dough. Knead well. Sprinkle flour on a board and then roll out dough until quite thin. Cut into strips. In skillet with hot, melted butter start dropping the dough strips one by one. Fry lightly until light brown. Drain well and serve hot. Serve with coffee and brandy.

Indispensable Hot Stuff

Salsa, that provocative, piquant tomato-based sauce, can be concocted in almost limitless variations and it also may be used to enliven and lend zest to an amazing number of dishes—which *might* help to explain why it has remained such an overwhelming California favorite down through the ages. Clearly, however, the main reason *salsa* has become a near staple in the Westerner's diet is its *taste:* tangy, peppery, and full of wonderful experimental surprises. Plain and simple—once its unique flavor is savored—the ingestion of *salsa* can become unashamedly habit-forming!

Curiously, however, *salsa picante* (or chili sauce, as it is generally known in the States) is *not* one of the delicacies imported from the mother-country of Spain by the aristocratic *hidalgos;* instead, it seems to have its roots in the exotic native cooking of Old Mexico. Most probably, the antecedent of *salsa* was *mole,* a sauce that the divergent but richly cultured Mexican Indian tribes used to spice their foods for centuries before the advent of the Conquest. This thick, dark sauce was a basic ingredient in the *tamal* (one of the very few foods of the truly ancient world to survive in its original form, giving infinite pleasure to our present-day palates); however, its primary use was as a tenderizer and garnish for the wild *juajolotl* (turkey), an abundant but tough, scrawny bird in those pre-Columbian times.

Surprisingly, *mole* can be found today on the menus of a few select Mexican restaurants throughout the Southwest, but, unlike the *tamal* (or, tamale, as it is commonly called in the States), *enchilada,* or *arroz* (rice) and *frijoles* (beans), the dark, seductive sauce has remained *the* prized secret among true gourmets of intricate Mexican cookery. Perhaps the mystery stems from the spectacularly unusual combination of ingredients to be found in *mole: chiles colorado* (hot red peppers), lard or oil, toasted bread crumbs, sugar, *anjonjolil* (toasted sesame seeds), *cacahuatl* (peanuts), *canela* (cinnamon), and—surely, the biggest surprise of all—*cacaotl* (chocolate)!

Salsa, as we know it, evolved sometime after the founding of Nueva Hispañola with the substitution of *tomatl* (red tomato) and *jitomatl* (green tomato) and *chiles verdes* (green peppers) in place of the more esoteric ingredients. Still, the adventurous cook is urged to add a pinch of *mole* (available in international food stores in paste form, which can be diluted with broth and prepared according to label instructions) to a favorite *salsa* recipe. We offer two highly individual and historic versions of the popular sauce.

SALSA SONOMA

In the first foreign language cookbook published in California (San Francisco, 1898), *El cocinero Españoli, obra que contiene mil recetas* (The Spanish Cookbook, a work that contains a thousand recipes), by Encarnación Piñeda, there appears a version of *salsa* that was a favorite of the famous Vallejo family. Honored guests from San Francisco and Sonoma were invited to relish large barbecues featuring beef and pork garnished with this legendary sauce. (The recipe has been modified for modern-day cooking.)

> 4 red-ripe tomatoes, diced
> 1 red onion, diced
> 1 green pepper, chopped
> 1 red pepper, chopped
> 1 teaspoon salt
> ½ teaspoon white pepper
> 1 teaspoon hot dry mustard
> 1 teaspoon celery seeds
> 2 tablespoons red or white garlic vinegar
> 2 tablespoons olive oil

Drain vegetables and put them in a mixing bowl. Add the seasonings and the garlic vinegar. Mix together, then add the olive oil. Mix again. Let stand in the refrigerator at least 4 hours before serving. AS A SIDE SAUCE, SERVES 6.

Hannah B. Lund, a fellow-cook of Charles Lummis, combined the cuisine of many cultures to perfection when she created a homemade California chili sauce that is *still* guaranteed to knock your socks off—just as it ignited the palates of Northern California ranch hands (*and* more than a few daring San Franciscans) in the early 1900s.

HACIENDA CHILI SAUCE

12 ripe tomatoes
12 green chili peppers
12 medium onions
3 cups sugar
3 cups cider vinegar
2 teaspoons allspice
2 teaspoons cayenne pepper
2 teaspoons salt

Wash and finely chop the tomatoes, chili peppers, and onions. Add all ingredients to a large saucepan. Boil together until thickened. Cool, store—and serve to a small army of hungry eaters.

A Pair of Definitive San Franciscans

San Francisco has been a center of the art of home economics for decades. In the 1940s and 1950s, two women reigned supreme in this category: Genevieve Callahan and Lou Richardson.

"Gen and Lou," as the pair were always affectionately called, knew "everybody" who was "anybody" in the city's tight group of dedicated food fanciers; together they created culinary trends that absolutely ruled the food and wine world of the West Coast.

Gen and Lou worked their gastronomical magic from two lovely locales—a sunny, airy apartment on Russian Hill and a delightful weekend cottage on the Inverness Peninsula. It's no overstatement to say that Genevieve Callahan understood California cookery better than anybody in her day, but, sadly, the marvelous cookbooks she produced, with Lou Richardson's help, are now out of print. Nevertheless, these books are remembered as benchmarks in the then "new" style that came to be known as California cuisine. Genevieve Callahan was not afraid to present cookery that was considered daring and even slightly scandalous; the liberal use of regional wine in her recipes caused quite a rumpus in those days!

What Callahan and Richardson accomplished in their field must surely have had a tremendous influence on their followers—culinary luminaries such as Dorothy Canet, Helen Evans Brown, James Beard, Emily Chase Leistner, and many more. Today's lifestyle periodicals offering comprehensive guides to Western cooking also owe them a great debt of gratitude.

One hopes that Genevieve Callahan—perhaps with a glass of local bubbly in hand, sharing a toast with Lou Richardson—is satisfied with what she helped to create when she smiles down on the city and state she loved so much. In her honor, we present her menu for an all-California dinner—a menu that has survived through the shared remembrances of those who had the privilege to sit at her table.

GEN AND LOU'S ALL-CALIFORNIA DINNER

California Fruit Cup
*(Sections of orange, pear, and peach in chilled passion fruit juice,
garnished with almonds and walnuts.)*

Broiled Chicken Halves
Mushroom Gravy
Steamed Rice
Buttered Artichoke Hearts

Ripe Olives   Celery
Large Bowls of Fresh Crab and Avocado
Louis Dressing

Chilled Chablis, Riesling, or Other White California Wine

Lemon Sherbet in Orange Shells
Crisp Raisin Cookies
Coffee   California Brandy

The Very Best

If all the attributes of San Francisco's superlative hostesses through the years could be manifested in a single woman, that woman would have to be the larger-than-life Phoebe Apperson Hearst.

Mrs. Hearst was married to the famous mine owner and entrepreneur George Hearst, and from the moment she set foot on the San Francisco shore as a young woman to the day she climbed the marble stairs at Buckingham Palace to be presented to Queen Victoria, Mrs. Phoebe Apperson Hearst was a definite *somebody*.

All society matrons in those days chose *one* night of the week during which they would "receive" for dinner; Phoebe Hearst chose to entertain at dinner at least *five* times a week. She looked upon those dinner parties as perfectly understandable, pleasurable obligations and her finesse as a hostess was unparalleled. Dozens of guests were invited to sit at her table every evening at the palatial Hearst mansion in San Francisco and a typical dinner for friends or business acquaintances could be described only as a royal feast: soup, fish, entrée, roast meat, fowl, salads, a variety of sweets and savories, several California cheeses, at least four wines (some chilled, some not), rich coffee, and, finally, a California brandy. In addition to the food and drink, the table settings and decorations were considered comparable to masterpieces.

When George Hearst decided to buck the social tide by purchasing an ancient *rancho* for a summer retreat in the less-than-fashionable county of Alameda in the East Bay (rather than the *then* much more fashionable North or South Bay), Phoebe Hearst refused to be thrown for a loop by the derelict, dilapidated condition of the adobe. She flew into action by hiring the talented designer and architect of San Simeon, Julia Morgan, and soon the tumbled-down *estancia* was transformed into a magnificent, romantic family ranch—the *Hacienda del Pozo de Verona*.

For the main house, Morgan fashioned a colonial-California work of art with a great fountain in the patio, pergolas, walled gardens *à la Córdoba*, hidden paths, and a Nun's Walk that was trellised with purple and white wisteria and bordered by Mrs. Hearst's favorite rose, the Cecile Brunner. Huge entertainments and fiestas were held at the hacienda; as an example of the vast architectural scope of the adobe, the Hearsts could easily accommodate over two hundred and fifty guests in the music room *alone* for an evening's gala.

Phoebe Apperson Hearst's charity work and contributions to the cultural life of the Bay area are the stuff of legend, but it is very possible that her status as *the* San Francisco hostess was her most enduring achievement. This great lady set a standard for *high* society that is still revered and meticulously observed today: *Start* at the top and *stay* at the top.

Sweet Herbs for Genteel Disturbances

A classic photograph published in San Francisco in the 1890s pictured a half-naked Indian peering intently at a sagebrush as if he were worshiping its very existence. If the spellbound native, who was a member of the Suisine tribe, venerated the common sage, it was with good reason: The Indians had discovered that chewing its leaves and swallowing its seeds was an effective cure for an infinite variety of ills, real or imaginary.

Soon after their arrival in Alta California, the Spanish colonists quickly learned about the efficacy of the redolent herb and, for generations, the basic Californiano remedy for minor ailments was sage tea, or *Cha*. This brew was absolutely guaranteed to cure colds, heal sore throats, and placate queasy tummies, just to name a few of its potent, miraculous qualities. *Cha* remained popular in San Francisco and the neighboring countryside until black tea was finally imported in quantity from China.

In a later chapter, we will introduce a variety of malevolent herbs that were used to squelch more serious and distasteful diseases—social or otherwise—but here we will concern ourselves with what was considered at the time to be domestic or "genteel" herbology as practiced by the homemakers of San Francisco. From *The California Recipe Book*, compiled by "The Ladies," we have this very gracious description of how to prepare sage tea:

CHA

A bouquet of sage leaves and other native herbs, tied in cheesecloth like a sachet.
A matching quantity of dried aromatic orange blossoms.
Lumps of crystallized rock candy.

Steep the bouquet in boiling water and then flavor the brew with a spray of orange blossoms. Sweeten the tea with lumps of crystallized rock candy.

There is a delightful story concerning an outing by the beauteous Maria de la Concepción Arguello, the daughter of the governor of the Presidio of San Francisco, to gather wild blackberries which, in 1806, grew in profusion. However, nothing much has changed; the blackberry continues to run rampant from countryside to city, triumphantly thriving even in vacant lots of San Francisco. "The Ladies" had a famous blackberry beverage recipe guaranteed to cool even the hottest day. They imbibed it "straight" (or so they claimed), but when served today as a modern spritzer (with club soda), the brew is still deliciously refreshing:

"THE LADIES'" BLACKBERRY SHRUB

> 2 quarts cider vinegar
> 4 quarts blackberries
> 1 quart sugar

Add the vinegar to the blackberries and let stand four days. Then strain the berries through a cloth without squeezing, and add the sugar to the juice. Boil for 20 minutes. Cool and serve over ice in a tall glass. (Will keep without sealing and should serve a bevy of modern "Ladies" very nicely.)

Of course, "The Ladies" realized that danger lurked everywhere and that the most innocent of pastimes could sometimes provoke nasty results:

CURE FOR POISON OAK
by
"A Lady" of Bush Street
Who Caught It While Picking Wild Blackberries

1 ounce gum shellac
6 ounces sulphuric ether
1 bottle with tight cork

Dissolve the gum shellac in the sulphuric ether; cork tightly in bottle until needed. Bathe the surface of the affected skin with cold water and wipe dry, then apply the bottled solution. The ether will evaporate in 1 minute, leaving a soothing coating of gum completely impervious to air. In about 2 minutes, the most distressing and painful cases of poison oak will be relieved. As the coating cracks and peels, apply more of the solution. In 24 hours, the source of indescribable suffering hopefully will be completely healed.

When the Spaniards dubbed a tiny island in the Bay, Yerba Buena, they paid tribute to the profusion of wild herbs growing on its slopes and throughout the Bay area. Though many of these plentiful wandering herbs have never become cash crops, they are still highly prized for their unique properties. As early as 1872, nasturtiums were considered San Francisco wild flowers by "The Ladies," who used the seeds for cooking to guarantee "a cooling of the stomach."

WILD NASTURTIUM SAUCE

1 cube butter
Flour, to cook's taste
Pickled Nasturtium Seeds

Melt the butter in a saucepan and add flour, which has first been diluted to a thin paste in water. When the sauce has boiled up and thickened, add nasturtium seeds that have been pickled simply by standing in cold vinegar.

"THE LADIES'" PICKLED NASTURTIUM SEEDS
(Capers)

Gather the nasturtium seeds and keep them for a few days on a paper tray. Then put them into empty pickle bottles and pour boiling vinegar over them. When the vinegar cools, cover the bottles tightly.

"THE LADIES'" NASTURTIUM SANDWICHES

To make nasturtium sandwiches, gather fresh nasturtium leaves and place them between slices of buttered toast. Place a light layer of mayonnaise on the leaves before serving. Garnish with nasturtium seed capers.

"The Ladies" were a font of delightful information—even when they described a potion for a rather vague, mysterious skin ailment:

PRESERVATION OF SEA MOSS

The color and consistency of dried seaweed may be preserved by brushing with the following solution: Dissolve 2 or 3 lumps of gum mastic in ⅔ cup of turpentine. Brush the moss with the liquid. Apply to afflicted area.

As we have seen, *The California Recipe Book* offered a highly unusual and diverse set of rules for domestic cures. However, there were other ladies who also used the indigenous herbs to prescribe potions for physical disturbances. In 1906, Mrs. Robert Dollar shared her recipe for liniment in the *San Rafael Cook Book:*

TO RELIEVE THE DREADFUL ITCH OF POISON OAK

Prepare a solution of equal amounts of ether, oil of juniper, spirits of camphor, and hartshorn. Rub it on the affected area.

If San Franciscans chose not to take the then-popular Krough's Head-ache Powders for "Head Ake" (as the advertisements read), then they could follow Mrs. R. L. Porter's advice as stated in her 1902 booklet *Crumbs from Everybody's Table.* These homemade remedies were considered as ordinary and worthwhile as aspirin.

MRS. PORTER'S RECIPES FOR THE SICK AND TROUBLED

BEEF ESSENCE

1 pound lean beef, diced fine
Wild onion to taste
Salt and pepper to taste

Place the meat in a heatproof jar without liquid. Cover the jar tightly and set it in a saucepan of cold water. Bring the water slowly to a boil and then reduce the heat to a simmer and continue heating until the juice of the meat is extracted and the meat fiber becomes colorless. Season to taste with wild onion, salt, and pepper.

BARLEY WATER

2 ounces pearl barley
½ pint boiling water
2 quarts water
¼ cup minced dried figs
¼ cup minced white raisins
Juice of 1 lemon
Dash of nutmeg
Sugar to taste

Place the barley in the ½ pint boiling water and let simmer for 5 minutes. Drain, and then add 2 quarts of water and bring the mixture to a boil. Add the figs and raisins. Then boil slowly until the liquid is reduced by one-half. Remove from heat, and then strain. Add the lemon juice, nutmeg, and sugar.

TOAST WATER

Take as many slices of toasted bread as you desire and cover them with boiling water. Let them steep in a covered dish until cold (but do not place them in the refrigerator). Strain off the water when cool and sweeten with sugar.

FLAXSEED LEMONADE

4 tablespoons whole flaxseed
1 quart boiling water
Juice of 2 lemons
Sugar to taste

Place the flaxseed in a mixing bowl. Pour the boiling water over the flaxseed and add the lemon juice. Cover and let the mixture steep for 3 hours. When cool, sweeten with sugar.

MULLED BUTTERMILK

1 pint buttermilk
1 egg yolk
1 teaspoon flour
Wild nutmeg to taste

In a saucepan, bring the buttermilk to a boil. Add the well-beaten egg yolk and the flour and allow the mixture to boil. Sprinkle with wild nutmeg. Serve hot.

There are many famous tonics that were created to promote general good health that did not include herbs or wild plants, of course. The following two recipes are such perfect examples of antidotes to the San Francisco fogs and chills that we were tempted to reproduce them anyway. Moreover, the cook is challenged to add a dash of a favorite California herb or spice. After all, it can't hurt, can it?

MRS. CONKLIN'S ANTI-FOGGER KOUMISS

1 quart milk
1 cup buttermilk
4 teaspoons sugar

Pour the milk into a mixing bowl. Add the buttermilk and the sugar and mix well. Be sure to completely dissolve the sugar. Put the bowl in a warm place and let the mixture stand 10 hours. By that time, it should be quite thick. Then pour the mixture from one mixing bowl to another until it becomes uniform in consistency. Bottle the koumiss and store it in a warm place for 24 hours in the summer and 36 hours in the winter. The bottle must be tightly corked, and the cork tied down. Shake well for 5 minutes before opening. Koumiss may be drunk as freely as milk.

MRS. FRANCIS HILLS' COLD DAY EGG NOG

6 tablespoons sugar
6 eggs
1 pint half-cream, half-milk
½ pint California brandy
¼ cup white rum

Beat the sugar and egg yolks together until well mixed. Beat the egg whites separately until very stiff. Mix the beaten yolk mixture with the cream-milk and fill 6 glasses half full with the liquid. In another bowl, mix the brandy and rum together and divide evenly among the 6 glasses. Cover this with the beaten egg whites. Stir lightly with a tiny spoon until the whites form into little nuggets. SERVES 6.

The Voodoo Witch of San Francisco

While the celebrated hostesses and homemakers of San Francisco were generally esteemed as women possessing the finest qualities of their sex—whether they specialized in entertaining, cuisine, or herbology—there was one notable and notorious exception to the genre. True, she *was* a celebrated hostess and user of herbs—but she was certainly *not* considered nice.

The formidable Mammy Pleasant will always be a part of San Francisco's lore, and whether the woman was as evil as reported or merely was a victim of heightened imaginations is a question we will leave to the biographers to unravel. However, the legend of the woman centers greatly around her supposed use of secret potions and deadly herbs. The reputed witch, so it is told, was famous for her cordials made from the wild clover that grew in profusion on Twin Peaks; her homemade, double-distilled elderberry and blackberry brandies were rhapsodized as the best in town—when served in a natural state and *not* as one of her deadly and infamous "Mickey Finns."

Mammy Pleasant was known to have had a large circle of gentlemen friends and they seemed to prefer a special drink while visiting their hostess, a brew called Balm Tea. This "tea" was believed to be liberally laced with a paralyzing gin. Perhaps it was no idle boast when Mammy Pleasant swore that she ". . . held the key to every closet in town with a skeleton in it . . . !"—information undoubtedly secured largely through an adroit loosening of an army of drunken tongues.

In 1853, John Walker introduced the eucalyptus tree to San Francisco. A decade or so later, Mrs. Pleasant had the fast-growing blue gums planted around all sides of her mansion at Bush and Octavia streets. Immediately, stories began to fly that the supposed witch within was working voodoo magic with the eucalyptus leaves. Many tales abounded, but one of the most interesting concerned a young, sick waif named Teresa Percy, whom Mrs. Pleasant virtually held captive inside the manor's tree-shrouded walls. It was whispered that the reason Mammy Pleasant could sustain so much power over her bewitched prisoner was that she could ease the pathetic Teresa's excruciating bronchial asthma with a foul drug processed from the eucalyptus leaf. Maybe, maybe not, but, to her own evil credit, it is said that Mammy Pleasant often gloated that she *always* got what she wanted—because she had a *way* with native herbs.

VI.
QUEEN CALIFA'S VIANDS

The Golden Gifts of Nueva Hispañola

When God looked down at the breathtaking site of one of the most beautiful bays in the world and said, *"Here*—build me a city," He also had the foresight to endow the land surrounding San Francisco with an awesome horn of plenty bursting with nature's edible riches. It's no wonder that the Conquistadores, traveling north from the dramatic, arid lands of the south and gazing at the huge, sparkling Bay with its lush countryside, felt justified in having named the land, north and south, *California*—in homage to the mythical Moorish Queen of the Caliphit.

Those early settlers did not *immediately* find the hidden gold that was prophesied to exist in Califa's paradise, of course; they found, instead, a treasure of viands and harvests. The natives' diet consisted of a bounty of grains, fruits, vegetables, and herbs, and these foods formed the basis of the early Spanish-American cuisine known as *Las comidas de California de antes*, or, Early California cookery.

Spanish-American cooking, its development rooted in over four hundred years of history, is the oldest bicultural cuisine in the Americas. The early Dons and their señoritas were quick to blend their style of cooking with that of the Indians of the West, as were their Hispanic compatriots on the East Coast. Such assimilation was relatively easy in the West and life continued to flow unhassled, mostly carefree, and essentially elemental mainly because of the abundance of food and land and the mildness of the weather. Until as late as the 1870s, the *estancias* consumed all that was grown within the boundaries of the *ranchos;* then, because of the ever-increasing bounteous harvests, "cash crops" began to develop as the *pobladores* discovered the true value of the rich land.

Later, even after the discovery of precious gold and while the miners and would-be merchants were brawling and whoring along the streets of "the city," the *ranchos* remained virtually untouched by such urbane antics. To visit the countryside in those days was a major undertaking; it meant hours in the saddle or being carted and jostled about in uncomfortable carriages over rutted, muddy roads. While San Francisco's super-sophisticated Palace Hotel was opening its gilded doors in 1875 to a cosmopolitan public, life at General Vallejo's Rancho Sonoma, for instance, remained unhurried and casual, just as it was at the start of the century.

Soon after, however, San Franciscans began to lust for "property." Fortunes were being made and the advantages of owning Northern California real estate were too obvious to be ignored. Besides, the *ranchos* provided the city's *haute monde* with a wonderful escape from the fogs and winds of a San Francisco "summer"—"going to the ranch" soon became a status symbol for the city's new millionaires. Some tried to steal the land and stories abound about their misadventures. A certain Irishman claimed ownership of Greater San Mateo County (then called Rancho de las Pulgas), but was soon thwarted by the law. Another decided that the Suisun Basin, located at the north end of the great Bay, belonged to him by divine right, but, he, too, was soon frustrated by local authorities. Many other fantastic claims were made and then denied by the court; Antonio Maria Osio was not satisfied with "owning" just any common piece of ground when he insisted that Angel Island (then known as Isla de Los Angeles), one of the jewels of San Francisco Bay, belonged to him; Joel Polack attempted to annex Yerba Buena Island before his efforts ended in failure.

Ironically, San Francisco's cultured citizenry were soon totally captivated by their "investment" properties in the valleys of Sonoma and Mendocino and Sacramento and San Joaquin, or on the rambling, ocean-fronted lands near Monterey and Carmel. And, equally ironic, when society's paragons journeyed to their *ranchos,* their lifestyles also changed, embracing a less hurried pace and a more simple cuisine—that of the Californianos.

The pattern reversed when, at the turn of the century and then between the two Great Wars and on, afterward, into the fifties, society's darlings religiously abandoned their *ranchos* in the country and their mansions in the city to enjoy "the season" in Europe. However, it seems the circle has finally closed. Today, with the worldwide recognition of California wines (which is spurring another "Gold Rush" to acquire lands in valleys and hills around the Bay area), the state's dynamic cultural brilliance, and the ever-increasing appreciation of California cuisine, the natives—and millions of yearly tourists—are quite content to remain and feast, both body and soul, at the gilded tables of Queen Califa's beautiful earthly kingdom.

The Californianos of Alta California

The typical day of a *patrón* (owner) on his *rancho* began at dawn with prayers and strong coffee. Then, at nine o'clock in the morning, it was time for his *almuerzo* (the first substantial meal of the day), usually consisting of the ever-present *tortillas*, *chorizo* (pork sausage with chili peppers), refried beans, goat cheese, and plenty of red wine and black coffee. After *almuerzo*, it was back to work for all hands, including the *patrón*.

Promptly at noon, bells announced the *comida de medio día*. Lunch would include *puchero*, a boiled stew, and a large salad made from home-grown greens. More red wine and more black coffee—and then off to blissful *siesta*. After waking and stretching, the *patrón* partook of the *merienda*, a light snack he would share with his *señora*, his family, and his guests. *La doña señora* (the lady of the house) always served the *merienda* herself, which could be a combination of dainties: herbal tea, short cakes, *agua fresca de naranja* (orange blossom water), and, perhaps, *dulce de membrillo* (quince preserve). Less delicate hands—the workers—ate ripe olives, cheeses, crisp corn chips, *cha*, chocolate or coffee.

On regular days, the *merienda* would replace the last meal of the day. Before retiring, the *patrón* and his circle might break open another bottle of wine—or two or three. On special days, however, such as saint's days or Sundays or days of cultural importance, the day usually ended with a *gran cena*. This huge supper featured much red meat, serious drinking, music, singing, and dancing. The next day . . . well, it would seem obvious after such a *fiesta*, that the next day would be greeted with an understandable chorus of pitiful moans and groans . . . !

The archetypical Californiano landowner could very well have been General Mariano Vallejo. His Northern California properties extended over fifty thousand acres and included his beloved Valley of the Moon in romantic Sonoma County. He raised sheep and cattle (and sold tallow and hides to the Yankees), and he cultivated wheat (which he sold to the Russians), barley, beans, and potatoes.

General Vallejo was also a governor of Alta California and one of his major talents was the art of entertaining important guests, many of whom sprang from the rarefied society of San Francisco. To this end, Vallejo built a lovely home at the base of an oak-studded hill in Sonoma, Lachryma Montis (The Tear of the Mountain), a lyrical name inspired by a clear spring of sparkling water that gushed its way down the nearby hillside.

Vallejo's *estancia* was a tapestry of green hues washed with sunshine. Laurel and oak trees dotted the acres; the fields, bisected by curving streams, were covered with a profusion of bright orange poppies (called "The Drowsy Ones" by the Indians because the flower closes its petals and hides from the night).

Lachryma Montis is now a state park and visitors are welcome. The rangers who guard the estate will sometimes reach for a round, yellow fruit from a giant pomelo tree standing near the doorway of the Vallejo house (the general imported many kinds of unusual, interesting, and little-known trees to adorn his *estancia*), and will slice a piece for the adventurous visitor to sample. A gracious gesture, surely, and one of which the general and his wife, *la doña señora* Benicia, would have heartily approved.

The *gran cena* at the Vallejo *rancho* contained many examples of interesting cooking that went far beyond merely barbecuing large slabs of meat. Some delicious examples are:

VALLEJO GARDEN *COLACHE*
(Succotash)

2 pounds pumpkin or summer squash
1 pound green string beans
2 tablespoons butter
1 onion, chopped
2 green chili peppers, chopped
2 large tomatoes, diced
1 clove garlic
Pepper to taste
Salt to taste
½ cup boiling water, if necessary
3 medium ears of fresh corn

Wash, peel, slice, and then dice the pumpkin; wash the beans and remove the strings. In a deep skillet, melt the butter, then add the pumpkin and beans. Lightly stir-fry. Add the onion, chili peppers, tomatoes, garlic, and the seasonings. Stir. Add ½ cup of boiling water if necessary, and simmer slowly until the beans are tender. Break the ears of corn into 2-inch lengths and add them to the skillet. Simmer for another 5 to 7 minutes. SERVES 6.

The native prickly pear cactus grew with abandon over the wild ridges of Sonoma Mountain, part of the Vallejo *estancia*. Cactus leaf joints were an essential food for the Gold Rush miners, and it was always a favorite of the Californianos. The leaves must be tender and free from thorns. (Cactus leaves, or *nopales*, can be purchased at international foods departments of most large supermarkets. The leaves usually are sold in glass jars.)

SONOMA MOUNTAIN CACTUS,
or *Nopales*

1 pound cactus leaves, young and thorn-free
1 teaspoon salt
Pepper to taste
2 tablespoons butter
1 onion, chopped
1 clove garlic
1 bay leaf
1 green chili pepper, chopped
2 tomatoes, sliced

Wash and cut the *nopales* into small pieces, then place in a saucepan of boiling water. Season with salt and pepper and cook until tender. Drain and set aside. In a large skillet, melt the butter, then add the onion, garlic, bay leaf, chili pepper, tomatoes, salt, and pepper. Fry together and then add the *nopales*. Sauté together for 15 minutes. SERVES 6.

As much as the early Californianos loved meat dishes, there was one meatless dish of which they thoroughly approved—a potato and chili casserole. Here is the way they made this attractive meatless dish at the Rancho Sonoma. They called it *tostones en chile*.

TOSTONES
(Potatoes in Chile Californiano)

12 red chiles
1 quart boiling water
1 tablespoon red or white garlic vinegar
2 tablespoons butter
1 tablespoon flour
1 tablespoon salt
2 cloves garlic, smashed
4 large potatoes
½ cup cooking oil

Preheat oven to 300 degrees F. Wash the chiles, wipe dry, and remove seeds and veins. Place chili peppers in 1 quart boiling water and cook until soft. Rub peppers through a sieve and then add the garlic vinegar to the pulp. Mix well and reserve. Melt the butter in a skillet and quickly brown the flour. Then add the salt, the garlic cloves, and the chile purée. Simmer for 15 minutes. Pare and cut the potatoes into ⅓-inch round slices. Heat the cooking oil (very hot) in another skillet and fry the potato slices until golden. Drain slices on paper towel. Fill a quart casserole with layers of potatoes alternating with layers of the chile purée. Cook for thirty minutes. The *rancheros* accompanied this dish with *cha*, the native herbal tea. DISH WILL YIELD 6 SERVINGS.

VALLEJO ORCHARD PERSIMMON SALAD

3 ripe persimmons
6 large leaves of butter lettuce
1 cup heavy cream
1 tablespoon horseradish
¼ teaspoon salt
½ teaspoon white pepper
Paprika, for garnish

Wash and cut the persimmons in halves, crosswise. Place each half in a lettuce cup. Whip the cream until stiff. Add the horseradish, salt, and pepper to the cream and stir well. Spoon the cream mixture on the persimmon halves. Garnish each half with dash of paprika. SERVES 6.

Among their large staff of kitchen helpers, the Vallejos employed Chinese, who planted their own grove of bamboo to provide the tender shoots so prized in their cuisine. The bamboo still grows where the Chinese workers placed the first roots.

VALLEJO KITCHEN CHINESE BAMBOO SHOOTS

To prepare bamboo shoots, use only the first 6 to 10 inches to appear above the ground. Remove the sheaths and soak in cold water for 30 minutes. Drain shoots and cut them into a desired length. Cook shoots 30 or more minutes in salted water until tender. Shoots of suitable age, when properly cooked, are always firm and rather crisp; they should never be soft or mushy. Bamboo shoots may be served with plain butter, butter sauce, or a basic cream sauce. Diced, the shoots make an interesting addition to salads. They may also be served in a Chinese-style sauce. (Precooked bamboo shoots may be purchased in large supermarkets.)

SAUCE FOR SUCCULENT BAMBOO SHOOTS

1 cup soy sauce
¼ cup water
1 tablespoon sugar
¼ teaspoon ground ginger
¼ teaspoon dry mustard

Mix all the ingredients together in a saucepan. Add the bamboo shoots to the sauce and simmer gently for ½ hour. Serve quickly.

A RELIC AND AN ALL-TIME FAVORITE

The common chick-pea, or garbanzo, was a daily staple on any Californiano's table; today, it's considered a rather esoteric salad filler or crunchy garnish. In the 1870s, however, the garbanzo was served as a main-course vegetable. For those who wish to turn back the clock to prepare the garbanzo from scratch (instead of relying on the canned, ready-to-serve variety), here is a wonderful recipe for an out-of-the-ordinary vegetable dish:

GARBANZOS *RANCHEROS*

2 cups dried garbanzos
2 tablespoons butter
1 teaspoon salt
Pepper to taste
1 onion, minced

Soak the garbanzos overnight, drain and then boil in fresh water until tender in a large saucepan. Drain the garbanzos and reserve the liquid. Heat the butter in a skillet and add the garbanzos. Simmer until tender. Then add the seasonings and the onion. Gently simmer for another 15 minutes. Then add 1 cup of the reserved liquid. Bring to a boil and serve hot as a vegetable. SERVES 4.

Though La Pérouse, the heroic navigator, introduced the potato to California in 1786, it has never replaced rice in the hearts and in the kitchens of California cooks. Rice is one of the many cereals native to North America and it was a staple in the diet of Indian tribes on both coasts. The Spaniards ate rice at almost every meal; that and the *tortilla* were "musts" in their diets. In modern times, California has become one of the major rice-growing regions of the world. The fertile acres that border the wide Sacramento River in the great Northern Valley (known to the Spaniards as "leagues") become a sea of green paddies for months on end, and—while San Francisco's restaurants offer a wide variety of rice dishes—Spanish Fried Rice remains an all-time favorite:

ARROZ DE CALIFORNIA ESPAÑOL DE ANTES

1 cup white long-grain rice
2 tablespoons olive oil
1 small onion, chopped
½ clove garlic, chopped
2 green chiles, chopped
2 ripe tomatoes, chopped
1 teaspoon salt
¼ teaspoon pepper
¼ teaspoon dried sweet basil
¼ teaspoon dried oregano

Preheat oven to 400 degrees F. Wash and drain 1 cup of long-grain rice. Heat the olive oil in a skillet and then add the rice. Fry lightly until rice turns a pale golden color; do not burn. Then add the onion, garlic, and the chiles. Sauté quickly together. When the onions are soft, add the tomatoes, salt, pepper, sweet basil, and oregano. Sauté lightly for another minute. Then place mixture in a deep-dish oven pan and cover the ingredients with boiling water. Put a tight cover on the oven pan and place the pan in oven to steam. Use a fork to stir occasionally, and keep the pan covered. The rice should be cooked dry and fluffy within 20 minutes. Do not overcook. SERVES 4.

Cures for Sinful Pleasures;
Poisons for Deadly Sins

Folklore has attributed negative and positive qualities to herbs since time immemorial. When the early settlers arrived in California, they found (as noted in a previous chapter) a plethora of wild herbs flourishing in the salubrious climate and rich earth—almost all of which, without a doubt, were imbued by the Indians with "good" or "bad" auras. Soon after their arrival, the *hidalgos* added a wide variety of European plants to the native herbal bonanza; added, also, were the inherent superstitions of "good" and "bad" attached to the new herbs.

The list of herbs considered "good" in that earlier era—plants whose main purpose was to enhance cookery or relieve misery from "genteel" maladies as lauded by "The Ladies of California" in their invaluable but quaint booklet—is almost endless. Cited are only a few examples:

Ájo (garlic)
Albahaca (sweet basil)
Anís (aniseed)
Bellotas (acorns)
Berro (watercress)
Bledo (wild amaranth)
Cebolla desierto (wild onion)
Chía (purple sage seed)
Chual (lamb's-quarters)
Cilantro (coriander)
Hinojo (fennel)
Lechuguilla (dandelion seed)
Lengua de vaca (sour dock)
Mostaza (wild mustard)
Oregano (wild marjoram)
Piñones (pine nut meats)

179

Popeta (miner's lettuce seeds)
Quelite sapo (frog greens)
Romero (rosemary)
Salvia (sage)
Tomillo (thyme)
Verdolagas (purslane or pigweed)
Yerba Buena (mint)

Just as important to the settlers as the "good" herbs, however, were the "bad" ones—those malevolent plants that were feared as the epitome of evil—because it was believed they cured or banished deadly sins and diseases hatched from sinful pleasures.

The South African-imported rose geranium, for instance, reputedly guarded against evil spells and protected against the "evil eye" when worn as an amulet in red cloth. A suspected witch could be warded off with a sprinkling of oregano (which, curiously, was considered both a "good" and "bad" plant and was known as "The Joy of the Mountain"); it could also be eaten or worn to "helpeth the nerves." The Dons and Doñas turned to peppermint to ease the pain of unful-filled love because they believed it dispelled the terrible "gnawing of the heart." Lemon balm was known to uplift the spirits. Toothache could be a killer in those days—dentists were few and far between, possessing questionable skills—and the Californianos chewed tarra-gon, named "The Little Dragon," to relieve the agony of rotting teeth. Manzilla (common camomile) was a sworn remedy for intense headaches. To banish earache, the Spaniards relied on an Indian cure: Laurel leaves were stuck in the ear—perhaps effecting a cure, but assuredly giving the sufferer a bizarre appearance, nevertheless.

The greatest fear of all, however, was malaria. In those days, the Sacramento River Delta and portions of the San Joaquin Valley were periodically invaded by hoards of poisonous mosquitoes, chiggers, gnats, and other vicious creatures that rose from the damp bogs. Gen-eral Vallejo was known to have contracted the disease, but he lived to talk about it. The early settlers had a very explicit, all-purpose cure for malaria: "Gorge oneself on *sandía* [watermelon] until stuffed for fevers!"

Sweet basil, considered the herb of love and hate, life and death, has had a remarkably interesting influence on the superstitious beliefs of Californianos, particularly San Franciscans. Most of the city's early Italian immigrants came from Genoa where there was a deep-rooted belief that basil was a protective agent against the bite of the basilisk, a mythical lizardlike monster. While there is no record of a single basilisk running amok in the streets of San Francisco, citizens *did* swear that the pungent herb could stop marauding witches dead in their tracks. Another oddity about basil concerns the manner in which it must be cultivated: In order to thrive, or so the legend goes, it must be periodically bombarded with curses and words of abuse!

Basil, like oregano, had a "bad" and a "good" aura; the "good" side of it was, and still *is* for most San Franciscans, its delicious appearance in Genoa's most popular dish, pasta with pesto sauce. In the old days, fresh basil could always be found in the city's green-grocer's stalls; today, the herb is stocked in the trendy supermarkets. There is even a basil newsletter, and the more fashionable Union Square shops advertise basil-colored garments. But, in the early days of settlement, the fragrant herb's greatest power was thought to be as an antidote to a new horror just being introduced from Asia: the feared and deadly wolfsbane.

In 1848, there were exactly *seven* Chinese males in Northern California. Mass migration began in earnest in 1849—the need for extra laborers became critical after the gold strike—primarily from the Kwang-tung Province in China. By 1854, it is estimated that there were 40,000 Chinese in the north of the state and, by 1876, the count was more than 152,000. The aspiring Asian laborers brought many magical potions to their new homeland, most of which were truly exotic and viewed positively by the Californianos. But the Asians allegedly brought one herb that was considered altogether frightful—the deadly wolfsbane. The plant was feared as being foremost in the lexicon of extremely effective oriental poisons. Since death was common as a result of myriad unknown causes and diseases and often came early to the residents of Alta California, there is no way to know how often wolfsbane was used for homicidal purposes, by whom, and for what reasons. There were always rumors, of course, that the horrible weed was the primary instrument of dispatch in the murky dens and underground tunnels of San Francisco's burgeoning Chinatown.

But the real magic imported by the Chinese, after their unique cuisine, perhaps, was their customs and cures. They blended their cultural habits with those of the Indians and the Spaniards, and California reaped the profits of yet another ethnic element. The Chinese, for instance, did not trust Western doctors (whom they called *Say Yee*) and relied, instead, on their own unique, vast medical lore of cures. To dispel loneliness and homesickness, it was a custom to add a pinch of Chinese soil (carefully carried from the fatherland) to a cup of tea and quickly swallowed. They considered nymphomania a form of spiritual intercourse, a heavenly state that—*if* absolutely necessary to cure—could be treated with powdered hartshorn. They believed, also, that flyswap was a symbol of purity; gold was the "Elixir of Life"; lapis one of the seven precious elements needed for a perfect life.

In 1918, while most of the state's population suffered severely from the worldwide influenza epidemic, San Francisco's Chinese community was left largely untouched by the killer bacteria—perhaps because they swore they consumed such huge quantities of citron melons.

It would take a thousand pages to make even the smallest dent in the Chinese lexicon of magical medicine and herbology. Here are some staple prescriptions as practiced in gaslight San Francisco's Chinatown—before conventional Western methods of curing began to supersede revered ancestral habits:

Sulphur	Kills worms and eases itching.
Bamboo tabisher	Puts new life into old sex.
Pomegranate blossoms and iron	To dye the hair.
Peacock's blood	Antidote for poisoning.
Bat dung	Cures diseases of the eye.
Powdered ivory	Speeds birth labors.
Fossil lizard teeth	Purifies the liver.
Ambergris	Promotes quick healing.
Mandrake	Produces a 2-day trance.
Powdered tiger bones	Helps end arthritis.
Bear galls	Ends stomach ache.
Cinnabar	Increases lifespan.
Gum of the *Koh-liu* from Sumatra	Acts as a general tonic.
Dandelion	Dispels bad breath.
Clove bark	Numbs toothache.
Honey	Eliminates cataracts.
Writing ink	Dissolves tumors of the eye.
Camboge	Causes teeth to fall out.
Magpie brains	Increases thinking power.

Magpie dung	Cures leprosy.
Turtle fat	Prevents hair from graying.
Turtle shells boiled in vinegar	Lowers fevers.
Extract of dandelion	Makes teeth grow.
Lily	Dispels grief.
	Promotes a male child.
	Eases the pain of piles.
White powdered jade	Increases bravery.
Jasmine	A general anesthetic.
Hot gold needles	Eases toothache.
Lapis	Cures inflammations.
Lavender water mixed with ink	Banishes headache.
Lotus	Eases the pain of childbirth.
	Makes old, wrinkled people have new, beautiful faces.
Mercury	Kills lice.
	Prevents prostitutes' conception.
Cinnamon with opium	Eases a withdrawal from drugs.
Fossil ivory	Cures bone diseases.

When the Cocktail Route Meandered
Through the Sylvan Countryside

Of the many wise dictums set down by the Chinese herbalists, there was one that seems to have been specifically tailored to cure the proverbial hangover of San Francisco's high-flying, gin-swilling *bons vivants:* "Boil the bark of poison oak and drink it for gin drinker's jaundice."

Did it work—or was it merely an example of excruciatingly painful instant suicide? Whichever, there's no doubt that the Gaslight Era sorely needed a cure for the so-called "Great Marin County Gin-and-Tonic Hangover." Our beloved sots were also invading the Peninsula in droves, perhaps seeking diversion from urban tedium and, when their jittery tummies permitted, relishing the countryside's innovative, intriguing cuisine.

Not all of the countryside's "new" settlers were puffy-faced immoralists, of course; the Bay area's finest families also were discovering the pleasures and profits of part-time living in the sylvan setting. For example, San Rafael and the neighboring Ross Valley were selected as vacation homesites by the wealthy Tobins, Livermores, Menzies, Dollars, and Boyds. "Going to the ranch," for some of the city's "Smart Set," meant traveling down the Peninsula to San Mateo and Santa Clara counties—even as far as the city of San Jose. Hillsborough, that quintessential millionaire's haven, perfectly suited the tastes of the Ralstons and the Burlingames. Fabulous mansions were built, many of which still stand today: the Fioli Mansion of the Matson-Roths; the Villa Montalvo of the Phelans.

Whether "high society" or just "high-living," the cosmopolitan invaders who set out east, north, or south from San Francisco encountered the heart of the state's richest agricultural lands. They feasted well at their summer *haciendas* and, to our eternal gratitude, took many of the pastoral recipes home to the city and preserved them for us to enjoy today. Bless those meanderers, one and all!

Fresh fruit pies are, primarily, an American invention; Europe's legacy consisted basically of pastry shells or layers filled with meats and wild game. Since the fruit crops of the North have yielded prize harvests for decades, it was obvious that vacationing San Franciscans would return to the city with unusual and provocative examples of fruit desserts. We have chosen these recipes which feature the famous California Bartlett pear and the spicy California Gravenstein apple:

MOUNTAIN BARTLETT PEAR PIE

Pie dough for 1 (9-inch) crust
4 cups thinly sliced, cored, peeled Bartlett pears
½ cup butter
1 cup sugar
2 eggs, beaten
1 teaspoon vanilla
4 tablespoons sifted flour
½ teaspoon salt
¼ teaspoon nutmeg
¼ teaspoon cinnamon
¼ teaspoon allspice

Preheat oven to 400 degrees F. Line a 9-inch pie pan with the prepared dough, and fill it to the rim with Bartlett pear slices. Cream the butter and sugar, mix in the beaten eggs and vanilla, and stir in the flour, salt, nutmeg, cinnamon, and allspice. Pour this mixture over the pears. Bake the pie for 15 minutes, then reduce the temperature to 350 degrees F. and continue baking until the crust is brown and the pears are tender. Cool the pie before serving. SERVES 6.

MOUNTAIN BARTLETT PEAR CAKE

2 cups sugar
½ cup oil
2 eggs, beaten
4 cups diced Bartlett pears
2 cups sifted flour
1 teaspoon salt
2 teaspoons cinnamon

                1 teaspoon allspice
                1 teaspoon nutmeg
                2 teaspoons baking soda
                1 teaspoon cream of tartar

Preheat oven to 350 degrees F. Thoroughly beat together the sugar, oil, and eggs. Then add the pears. In another bowl, sift the flour and resift it with salt, cinnamon, allspice, nutmeg, baking soda, and cream of tartar. Stir this into the pear mixture with minimal strokes, and pour the batter into a 9 × 13-inch greased pan. Bake the cake for at least an hour, or until it tests done. Dress the cake with vanilla-flavored icing. SERVES 8.

The earliest Bohemian Clubbers traveled the beautiful Gravenstein Highway, trekking through Marin County on what is now Highway 101 to the Sonoma County turn-off near Santa Rosa, to reach their famous Bohemian Grove at Monte Rio in the secluded Russian River country—as members still do. A distinctive apple butter, made from these "apples with character," was served at the Bohemian Club around 1900.

BOHEMIAN GROVE APPLE BUTTER

                12 pounds Gravenstein apples
                2 quarts fresh Gravenstein apple cider
                6 cups sugar
                21 teaspoons cinnamon
                12 teaspoons powdered cloves
                6 teaspoons allspice
                4 tablespoons ground lemon peel
                Juice of 4 lemons
                2 cups Madeira wine

Wash, remove the stems from the apples, and quarter them. Reduce the fresh cider by cooking it down to half its original quantity. Bring the apples and the cider to a boil and then reduce heat and slowly simmer the apples until soft. Strain the mixture, and add sugar. Stir thoroughly, and add cinnamon, powdered cloves, allspice, ground lemon peel, lemon juice, and Madeira. Cook mixture for 2 hours over low heat, stirring occasionally until the butter is thick. SERVE ON BISCUITS, CRACKERS, OR TOAST.

The Gravenstein apple country was just around the corner from Guerneville. Summer campers were known to have served an invention named "McGinty's."

McGINTY'S APPLES

1 pound dried Gravenstein apples
1 cup loosely packed brown sugar
1 teaspoon vanilla
1½ tablespoons cinnamon
½ teaspoon nutmeg
Prepared piecrust mix for 2
    (9-inch) crusts

Preheat oven to 450 degrees F. Wash and remove core and skins from apples. Soak apples overnight in cool water. Next morning, replenish enough water to stew apples in large kettle. Cook apples until soft, blend together with a spoon, and then return to heat. Add brown sugar and vanilla, then cook until the mixture is thick. Cool, and then add the cinnamon and nutmeg. Line a pie pan with 1 prepared piecrust. Pour mixture into the pie dish. Cover mixture with second piecrust, and then prick a few holes in the crust with a fork. Bake until crust is golden, and then reduce heat to 350 degrees F. and bake until filling is cooked. SERVES 6 TO 8.

When traveling to Sacramento from San Francisco by steamer— the easiest and smartest way to reach the capital in bygone days— the ship floated past orchards of apricots and many other fruit trees. This delicious dessert comes from a Sacramento grower's grandmother, a native daughter of the Golden West:

SACRAMENTO SUNSHINE

1 cup apricot jam
¼ teaspoon salt
1 cup stiffly whipped cream
Glacé fruit, to cook's taste, for garnish

Beat the jam until soft and smooth, then blend in the salt. Fold in the stiffly whipped cream. Pour mixture into a refrigerator tray and freeze 4 hours or more. Before serving, garnish with glacé fruits. MAKES 1½ PINTS.

Over the hills near Santa Cruz, Judge J. H. Logan developed a California treasure—the loganberry. He reportedly created the rather tart fruit from the Western dewberry and the common blackberry. Judge Logan announced his discovery in 1881, and the berry enjoyed a tremendous popularity and was the chic dessert up and down The Peninsula.

On the opposite side of the far-reaching Bay, Luther Burbank created another berry—the Phenomenal. Burbank's mutant made use of Logan's dewberry, but crossed with the raspberry rather than the wild blackberry. Both berries made an excellent dessert sauce, but we present Burbank's creation:

THE PHENOMENAL DESSERT SAUCE

1 cup sugar
2 tablespoons butter
1 tablespoon cornstarch
1 teaspoon vanilla extract
½ cup cold water
½ cup berry juice

Cream the sugar and the butter, and then add the cornstarch mixed with the vanilla and cold water. Gently boil for 5 minutes. Stir constantly. Add the berry juice and cook mixture for another 5 minutes. Cool. SERVE OVER ICE CREAM. MAKES ABOUT 1½ CUPS.

The elegant avocado has been highly prized by Westerners since the time of its importation. Very early on, the aristocratic fruit was known as the Alligator Pear from California. The sometime chef of the old Mark Hopkins Hotel, the formidable Joseph Meyer, created this marvelous sauce to grace the lemony-green pear.

AN ELEGANT SAUCE FOR THE CHIC AVOCADO

> 4 teaspoons mayonnaise
> 2 teaspoons chili sauce
> 1 tablespoon basic French dressing
> 1 teaspoon finely minced shallots
> Touch of garlic, to cook's taste
>
> 2 avocados
> 1 large lemon, sliced, for garnish

Blend the ingredients together well and chill. Serve over freshly peeled and diced avocados in crystal cocktail tumblers. Garnish with lemon slices. SERVES 4.

Almonds came to California in the gunnysacks of the good *padres* during the sixteenth century. In the 1800s, society ladies savored almond candy at teatime.

GAZEBO TEA ALMOND ROCHA

> 1 pound butter
> 2 cups sugar
> 1 cup chopped almonds
> 1 teaspoon vanilla

Melt the butter in a saucepan, add the sugar, almonds, and vanilla. Cook without stirring until the mixture becomes medium brown. Do not overcook or burn. Then turn the mixture into a buttered pan. After it cools and hardens, break into pieces and serve. SERVES 6 TO 10.

On their way to the Monterey Peninsula, our birds-of-summer habitually stopped overnight at Half Moon Bay or other fog-shrouded hamlets on the Pacific shore. The silver-gray artichoke thrived in the region's chilly climate and was featured on menus all along the coast. Breakfast-before-leaving in picturesque inns was a delight—then and now.

HALF MOON BAY BOARDINGHOUSE ARTICHOKE SCRAMBLED EGGS

2 hearts of artichoke, cooked
1 tablespoon butter
1 clove garlic, minced
1 small onion, minced
2 or 3 eggs, to cook's choice
Fresh parsley sprigs, chopped, for garnish

Quarter the artichoke hearts. Melt the butter in a skillet, then add the artichoke hearts, garlic, and onion. Sauté the mixture until onions are soft. Beat the eggs in a bowl, then add to skillet. Scramble until done. Garnish with parsley and serve at once. SERVES 1.

This homey version of eggs, chicken, and ham in a white sauce has, unfortunately, fallen out of vogue. A hearty, old-fashioned egg dish, the recipe deserves to be remembered as it was served by a Cloverdale family in the early 1900s:

MENDOCINO EGGS

8 hard-boiled eggs, sliced
1 heaping cup diced, cooked ham
1 heaping cup diced, cooked chicken
½ cube butter
½ cup bread crumbs
Basic Cream Sauce for Mendocino Eggs
Buttered toast

Preheat oven to 350 degrees F. Arrange the eggs, ham, chicken, butter and bread crumbs in layers in a buttered casserole. Pour the cream sauce over the ingredients and bake until mixture is thoroughly heated. Serve immediately over buttered toast. SERVES 6.

BASIC CREAM SAUCE FOR MENDOCINO EGGS

2 tablespoons butter
4 tablespoons flour
Salt to taste
White pepper to taste
2 cups milk

Melt the butter in saucepan over low heat. Add the flour and seasonings and stir into the butter. In another saucepan, bring the milk almost to a boiling point. Then add the milk all at once to the flour mixture, stirring constantly until thickened. Simmer for 3 to 5 minutes. MAKES 2 CUPS.

The following recipes feature California favorites from appetizers to sassy spinach:

ROSS VALLEY APPETIZER

Fresh pomegranate seeds
Chopped filberts
Honey

"Pick the pomegranates from your own tree," a helpful Ross Valley matron advised, being perfectly serious. If you don't have your own tree, try the local supermarket. Remove the seeds from the pomegranates and mix them with chopped filberts to which has been added just enough honey to moisten. Serve in small bowls as an appetizer or first course. Servings should be tiny. Adjust quantity of ingredients for the number of guests.

SANTA CLARA MISSION SWEET POTATOES

6 sweet potatoes
1 tablespoon butter
½ teaspoon salt
¼ teaspoon nutmeg
½ cup heavy cream
½ cup chopped walnuts
16 marshmallows

Preheat oven to 375 degrees F. Peel and boil sweet potatoes until tender. Drain, mash with butter, salt, nutmeg, and cream. Fold in walnuts. Spread mixture in a greased square cake tin, lay on the marshmallows, and bake until bubbly brown. SERVES 6 AS A SIDE DISH.

SAN RAFAEL CUCUMBER SAUCE

4 large cucumbers
½ cup heavy cream, whipped
1 teaspoon white pepper
1 teaspoon salt
1 onion, minced
2 teaspoons white tarragon vinegar

Peel and grate the cucumbers and put pulp in a large bowl. Refrigerate. When chilled, add the whipped cream and remaining ingredients and blend well. Delicious over cold salmon. MAKES ENOUGH SAUCE FOR 6 SERVINGS.

CHARLES LUMMIS' *COLACHE*
"Stockton Pumpkin Surprise"

1 tender, young pumpkin
½ cup cooking oil
Salt to taste
2 medium tomatoes, diced
1 large onion, chopped
2 cloves garlic, minced
1 bell pepper, chopped
1 heaping tablespoon butter

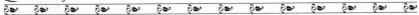

Wash the pumpkin, remove the seeds, and prepare 1 quart of the meat, cubed. Sauté the cubes in oil in a large skillet for 5 minutes. Add salt and stir often. Put the rest of the ingredients in pan, cover, and cook over slow heat for 45 minutes. SERVES 4 AMPLY AS SIDE DISH.

PAJARO RANCH PEPPERS

6 large bell peppers
Salt
½ pound cooked bay shrimp
1 tablespoon finely chopped celery
1 cup bread crumbs
Ground pepper to taste
½ teaspoon dry mustard
1 egg
1 tablespoon butter

Preheat oven to 375 degrees F. Rinse and dry the peppers. Cut off the stems and remove the seeds from the peppers. Place in cold, salted water for ½ hour. Mix together the rest of the ingredients and stuff the peppers with the filling. Place peppers in casserole and bake for 20 minutes. SERVES 6 AS A SIDE DISH.

Because of the Bay area's cultural mix of peoples, many kinds of unusual greens are to be found fresh at the grocer's. Often a particular variety will be recognized only by the ethnic population to whom it is familiar and indigenous. In the golden days, edible greens grew nearly everywhere in the north and were regularly picked for food. These wild plants were called *quelites*, or cooked greens. Blooms of yellow mustard still grace the hills of Marin County, the Deep Peninsula, and the towering slopes of Mount Tamalpais. Another favorite still growing wild is Swiss chard. Cooked or steamed just slightly to retain its crispness and full flavor, chard can be a delicious side dish. In the Italian restaurants of San Francisco, chard is fried lightly in olive oil and then served to complement fresh fish. Today, spinach often takes the place of the more exotic wild varieties:

CALIFORNIA SPINACH

2 pounds fresh spinach
2 cups boiling water
½ teaspoon salt
2 tablespoons olive oil
2 green onions
1 clove garlic

Wash the spinach leaves. Then place the spinach in a saucepan with 2 cups of boiling water and season with salt. Quickly steam tender, then drain and chop fine. Heat the olive oil in a skillet. Mince onions and garlic and add to oil. Constantly stirring, sauté for 1 minute. Then add chopped spinach and gently simmer for 4 minutes. Serve hot as a side dish. SERVES 4.

VII.
FANCIFUL FOOD PURVEYORS
TO A GOLDEN CITY

THE CLEVER FIRST-FAMILIES WHO OPENED BUSINESSES TO KEEP SAN FRAN-cisco in food and drink couldn't help but make fortunes, perhaps even more than all the gold taken from the Mother Lode. Nor could they have selected a more lucrative location to market and process their assorted products. With some of the richest agricultural land in the world in Northern California, these enterprising commercial pioneers did not lack the best raw material. And what wasn't grown nearby was quickly imported; the then bustling port of San Francisco was the busiest in the West.

Some of the best-known brand names that date from the Golden Era have disappeared or are no longer as widely distributed in the retail market. Still, other brands continue to be marketed throughout the modern world. These early businessmen gave impetus to the growth of downtown trading sections collectively known today as "California Street," the blocks that surround the intersection of California and Market streets. Altogether, more canned and fresh commodities change hands within the confines of this square-mile area than in all the similar markets of any other Western country. Now that California wines have earned such a marvelous worldwide acceptance, the "reds and whites" have become staples for these traders.

The California Street Lunch, which originated shortly after the city was reconstructed, was either famous or infamous, depending on one's particular point of view. It typically lasted from two to five hours and involved two-fisted drinking and belly-bulging eating. No wonder the red-faced participants were rarely expected back at the office after such a repast!

These purveyors shaped San Francisco's inspired cuisine. We have included some of their most celebrated traditional recipes.

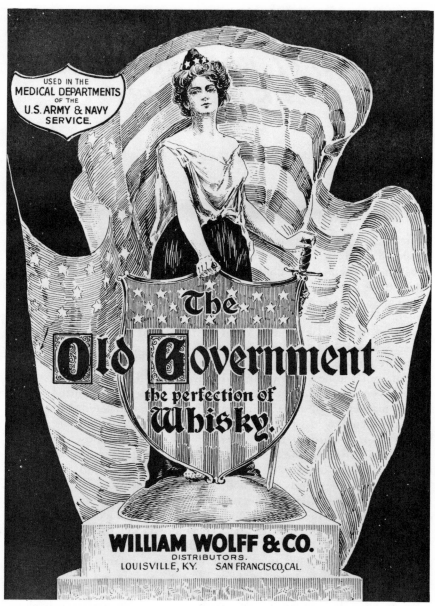

WILLIAM WOLFF & COMPANY, the distributor of Pommery wine
in San Francisco

Photo courtesy of the Department of Special Collections, Shields Library

S & W

A San Francisco Institution

S&W Fine Foods, very much in existence today as part of a large grower-owned cooperative, has represented superb quality for more than one hundred years. Happily, San Franciscans were the first to savor its products, but now the initials are known to nearly everyone. And, yes, there most certainly was a Mr. *S*ussman and a Mr. *W*ormser. About 1904, S&W published a *Greenbook of Recipes* that included two versions of homemade tomato soup and instructions for a marinated Viennese chicken.

TOMATO SOUP

1 (16-ounce) can plain tomatoes, with juice
1 scant teaspoon baking soda
1 quart very hot milk or 1 cup heavy cream
1 tablespoon butter
Salt and pepper to taste
Fine cracker meal, to cook's touch
Hot buttered crackers, if desired

Heat the tomatoes with their juice and force them through a strainer into a medium saucepan. Add the scant teaspoonful of baking soda. When it stops effervescing, add the hot milk or heavy cream, and the butter. Then add salt and pepper to taste, stirring constantly, and thicken with cracker meal. Serve with hot buttered crackers, if desired. SERVES 4.

TOMATO BISQUE

1 (16-ounce) can plain tomatoes with juice, chopped into small
  pieces
1 tablespoon butter
½ onion, diced
Salt and pepper to taste
1 quart milk
Dash of baking soda
1 tablespoon cornstarch in a little milk
Canned shrimps, drained and cut in small pieces, to cook's touch
2 hard-boiled eggs, chopped

In a large saucepan, boil together the tomatoes, butter, and onion
for ½ hour. Strain the soup, return to saucepan, and then add salt,
pepper, and the milk to which the baking soda has been added.
Thicken the soup with the cornstarch dissolved in milk, stirring
the pot for several minutes until thoroughly heated. Before serving
the soup, add shrimps and chopped, hard-cooked eggs. Heat again.
SERVES 4.

VIENNA CHICKEN IN OLIVE OIL

1 large stewing chicken, cut into pieces
Juice of 1 lemon
Olive oil
Fresh parsley, chopped, to cook's touch
1 bay leaf
Salt and pepper to taste
2 eggs, beaten
1 cup bread crumbs
1 cup chicken stock
1 cup heavy cream
1 egg yolk
10 button mushrooms

The marinade that flavors this chicken must originally have been
intended to tenderize an older bird. If you don't have an old bird
to cook, substitute a fryer for the stewing chicken.

Marinate the chicken for 3 hours in lemon juice and olive oil, with some parsley, the bay leaf, and salt and pepper. Drain the pieces and dry them, then dip each one into the egg, then the bread crumbs. Fry them until golden brown in more olive oil. In a saucepan, mix the stock with the cream, egg yolk, and mushrooms. Season this mixture and simmer it, stirring until it thickens. Add more chopped parsley and a little extra lemon juice, and serve the chicken with the sauce poured over it. SERVES 4 TO 6 AS AN ENTRÉE.

This recipe for a French lamb stew, while not from the S&W booklet, calls for several canned commodities made by the firm. A distinguished mercantile San Francisco family has served this stew to guests for generations, often preceded by Celery Victor (see Part II, Victor Hirtzler).

PACIFIC HEIGHTS FRENCH LAMB STEW FOR COMPANY

2 tablespoons butter
½ cup chopped onions
2 cloves garlic, crushed
2 pounds boneless lamb, cubed
3 tablespoons flour
1 cup chicken stock
1 cup dry sherry
2 teaspoons Worcestershire sauce
½ teaspoon paprika
Salt and white pepper to taste
1 (8-ounce) can small onions, drained
1 (8-ounce) can petite peas, drained
1 (3-ounce) can mushroom caps, drained
4 carrots, chopped and cooked
1 cup sour cream
Fresh parsley sprigs, for garnish

Heat the butter in a large skillet, and sauté the onion and garlic until they are tender and transparent, but do not brown. Remove them from the pan and reserve them. Add the cubes of lamb to the pan and brown them lightly. Sprinkle the meat with the flour and add the chicken stock and dry sherry. Stir this mixture until the sauce thickens. Then add the Worcestershire sauce, paprika, salt, and white pepper, and the reserved onion and garlic. Cover the pan tightly, and simmer the stew 1½ hours, or until the meat is tender. Add the canned onions, peas, and mushrooms and the cooked carrots and heat them through. Stir in the sour cream, taking care that the stew doesn't come to a boil again. Serve the stew garnished with sprigs of parsley. SERVES 4 TO 6 AS AN ENTRÉE.

Sperry Products

Going, Going, Gone—
"And Sold to the Flour Sack!"

Sperry's Drifted Snow Flour was San Francisco's favorite. After all, the Sperry Products was started by San Franciscans for San Franciscans. Those who remember it fondly no doubt regret that General Mills, which bought the company, discontinued the brand locally. In the 1900s, Sperry published a series of small booklets in paper wrappers with recipes using their flour. Collectors of cookbooks consider them to be *priceless*, and they are to be found in only a handful of special collections in public and private libraries. We have rediscovered a few of them, and several of the more select recipes have appeared throughout this book.

While we are proud of the fact that Sperry Flour originated in our town, and we know that the company had a creditable history, we are much more fascinated by Miss Beth Sperry, the sister-in-law of the powerful and enormously rich William H. Crocker, "Bonanza King of Snob Hill." In the early 1890s, the San Francisco *Examiner* reported that seven California girls who were at the top of the social scale married seven shabby shopworn princes, counts, or earls, acts that cost their families nearly twenty million dollars. In 1895, William H. Chambliss, a relative nobody, shocked San Francisco society by having printed in New York a scurrilous book, *Chambliss' Diary; or, Society As It Really Is*. Within its covers, he told the whole story, listing the girls, the noblemen, and the amounts of money. The town's millionaire matrons had a collective stroke and desperately attempted to have the embarrassing book suppressed. When the book hit the stands in the Bay area, swarms of hysterical matrons representing the cream of society fell upon the bookstores and bought all the available copies to have them later destroyed. Chambliss' wicked little book became an instant "hot ticket"; thanks to those outraged mothers and aunts, it still remains a "hot" and most elusive item to obtain even today.

But Chambliss especially "had it in" for the Crockers. He accused
W. H. Crocker of having purchased Prince Andre Poniatowski for
Beth Sperry as a "Fourth-of-July" present. On balance, it seems to
have been a perfectly nice gesture—the prince was said to have cost
only two hundred and fifty thousand dollars. This was a piddling
sum compared to what Eva Julia Mackay's daddy was alleged to have
paid for Prince Colonna: a sweet five million! Still more grist for
Chambliss' mill was the fact that poor Prince Poniatowski was a
reject, several times over. He had offered himself, it was reported,
to Horace Carpentier, the Oakland financier whose niece, Maud
Burke, was said to be heatedly looking for a title. But, instead, mysteri-
ously, the Oakland heiress became Lady Bache-Cunard for somewhere
in the neighborhood of two million dollars. Despite what Gertrude
Stein said about Oakland, there must have been *some* "there" *there*.

For some strange reason, the only available titles of the day were
either Polish or Russian. The very best was considered to be a "high"
Russian title with a family seat somewhere in the general vicinity
of St. Petersburg. God forbid the candidate should be from the Lower
Caucasus! And, most horrible of all, unless the likely husband was
a Radziwill or a Potocki, it would never, never *do* to be a Polish
prince. It is not known whether Prince Andre Poniatowski was a
"higher" or "lower." The poor fellow couldn't have been all *that*
bad, as he and some of his associates founded Tanforan Racetrack.
Perhaps he was a "higher" after all. But Chambliss was not to be
denied his description of "Penniless Prince Poniatowski's Society
Auction Sale." As part of a cruel caption to a cartoon, Chambliss
had the unfortunate prince declaim, "How much am I offered for
myself, my gall, and my empty title? First, second, third and last
call—and sold to the flour sack!"

One of the Sperry booklets gives us the genuine recipe for Lady
Baltimore Cake, reserved for only very important, very special occasions.

LADY BALTIMORE CAKE

1 cup butter
2 cups sugar
3½ cups flour

3 level teaspoons baking powder
1 cup milk
1 teaspoon rose water
6 egg whites, beaten stiff
Lady Baltimore Frosting

Preheat oven to 350 degrees F. Cream the butter and gradually beat in the sugar. Sift together the flour and baking powder, and add this to the butter and sugar alternately with the milk and rose water. Last, fold the egg whites into the batter. Pour it into 3 well-buttered pans and bake the cake about 40 minutes or until it springs back lightly to the touch. Cool 10 minutes in pans, then remove layers from pans. When they have cooled, fill the layers and cover the top with Lady Baltimore Frosting. SERVES 6 TO 8.

LADY BALTIMORE FROSTING

3 cups sugar
1 cup boiling water
3 egg whites, beaten stiff
1 cup chopped raisins
5 figs, sliced
1 cup chopped nutmeats

In a saucepan, heat the sugar and water, stirring them until the sugar is dissolved, then let the syrup boil without stirring it until it will spin a long thread from a spoon. Pour this over the egg whites, beating the frosting until it is cold. Add the fruits and nuts, and spread the frosting between the layers and on top of a Lady Baltimore Cake.

Eleanor McClung McMurran introduced the Lady Baltimore Cake to her Belvedere and San Francisco circle of friends. "Aunt Nell," as she was affectionately called, got the recipe from her friend Mrs. Woodrow Wilson. The cake was a great favorite with the Wilsons. It is told that Mrs. Wilson liked to hide "treasures" for her husband to discover among the layers of the cake. If this little tale is true, it must have been a miracle that our late President didn't break every tooth in his mouth!

Goldberg, Bowen

A Fancy-Food Treasure House

Jack Goldberg came to San Francisco in the 1850s, lured to make the trip across the plains from Kansas by the promising commercial possibilities of the Gold Rush. In 1868, he and a partner bought the pioneer Kroenig grocery store, and the firm subsequently merged with the Bowen Brothers to become Goldberg, Bowen & Company. Of their several locations, the Post Street store was the most famous, stocked with all sorts of fancy foods, imports, candies, gifts, and exotics. The firm was the first gourmet grocery store in our city, a worthy predecessor of today's Oakville Grocery.

In those vigorous days, to take a noontime tour of the grocery's first floor was thought to be a great way to while away a lunch hour. A few years later, when food began to be served, it became a favorite lunch spot for everybody from the mailroom boy to a managing director. For many years, the eccentric chairman of one of San Francisco's original advertising agencies used its premises to hire and fire his staff. To be hired by this media magnate meant that one lunched with him at Goldberg, Bowen to consummate the deal. On the other hand, "Black Friday" was a horrible reality for those at the agency about to be fired. Thursday evening, the timid chairman would depart for Los Angeles on the Southern Pacific Lark; his hatchet-man assistant was left behind to do the dirty work. The unknowing victim would then be commanded to appear at a Friday lunch on the balcony with the insidious executioner. It is a wonder that some of those unfortunates did not throw themselves off the high, inside second-story balcony, to land ingloriously amid the pretty display below of Dutch hams and guava jellies.

However, Goldberg, Bowen is best remembered for its lovely aura of frivolity and adventure. Many a tender romance began over lunch in this restaurant, and, even in those more delicate days, many a couple did not immediately return to work after a discreet tête-à-tête. . . .

In 1891, Goldberg, Bowen distributed *Home Dissertations*, a cookbook written by a Mrs. Tilton. Veal, the most epicurean of all meats, was an obvious favorite of the author; these three recipes are Mrs. Tilton's.

ROAST FILLET OF VEAL

    1 medium-size veal roast
    ½ cup bread crumbs
    ½ cup finely chopped salt pork
    Salt and pepper to taste
    Marjoram, to cook's touch
    ¼ cup beef broth or water
    2 tablespoons flour, lightly browned in a dry skillet

Preheat oven to 350 degrees F. Remove the bone from the veal roast, and spoon into the cavity bread crumbs seasoned with chopped salt pork, salt, pepper, and marjoram. Make deep cuts in the veal and fill these, too, with the stuffing; then bind the fillet closely with twine. Roast, keeping a little water or broth in the roasting pan, and baste the meat often until it is thoroughly done. Remember, no one likes rare veal. To make the gravy in the dripping pan, pour off the excess fat, add broth or more water, if necessary, and season to taste with salt and pepper. Thicken the gravy with brown flour and serve with the roast. SERVES 4 TO 6 AS AN ENTRÉE.

VEAL CUTLETS

    1 medium-size veal round
    2 egg yolks, beaten
    Salt and pepper to taste
    1 teaspoon grated lemon peel
    Nutmeg to taste
    ½ cup bread crumbs
    3 tablespoons butter
    1 cup hot water
    2 tablespoons seasoned flour
    1 tablespoon lemon juice
    1 lemon, sliced, for garnish

Cut 1-inch-thick slices from the veal round. In a frying pan, half-cover the meat with boiling water; cover the pan closely and let the meat simmer for 10 minutes. Drain and dry the meat, and dip the pieces in the beaten egg yolks seasoned with salt, pepper, grated lemon peel, and a little nutmeg. Then roll the pieces in the bread crumbs. Sauté them in butter. When the veal is cooked, remove it from the pan and pour out nearly all the fat. Add instead 1 cup of hot water, and thicken this with seasoned flour, stirring up the crusty bits and adding a little lemon juice. Pour gravy over the veal and garnish the dish with sliced lemon. SERVES 4 TO 6 AS AN ENTRÉE.

STUFFED SHOULDER OF VEAL

1 medium-size shoulder of veal roast
½ cup bread crumbs
Dried thyme to taste
Fresh parsley, to taste, chopped
Nutmeg to taste
1 tablespoon butter
1 tablespoon beef suet
Cooked pork fat or ham, if desired
Milk or hot water, to cook's touch
Salt and pepper to taste
4 tablespoons flour
12 medium potatoes, peeled
Fresh parsley sprigs, for garnish

Preheat oven to 400 degrees F. Remove the bone from a shoulder of veal roast without cutting through the outer skin. Spoon into the cavity a stuffing of bread crumbs, thyme, parsley, a little nutmeg, butter, beef suet, and if desired, the pork fat or ham—all moistened with milk or hot water. Sew the cavity closed, restoring the shape of the shoulder. In the hot oven, roast it, resting on the bone, to a golden brown. At this point, remove the roast from the oven and reduce the heat to 350 degrees F. Season the roast with salt and pepper, dredge it with flour, and baste it with the drippings from the pan. Then bake the veal again, this time in a slow oven (300 degrees F.) about 20 minutes for each pound. About 45 minutes before the roast is done, add the potatoes to the pan with the veal; turn them occasionally to ensure even roasting. When the meat is done, serve it surrounded by the potatoes on a platter garnished with more parsley. SERVES 4 TO 6 AS AN ENTRÉE.

Ghirardelli

Dream Cookies of 1900

Per capita, San Francisco consumes more chocolate chip cookies than any other city in the United States! As the new century began, the D. Ghirardelli Company asked Frank Bok, then pastry chef at the Palace Hotel, to create a series of desserts using their chocolate and cocoa. Chef Bok's recipes, published in *Dainty Dessert Dishes*, come from that wonderful faraway time when the company really did produce chocolate at Ghirardelli Square.

CHOCOLATE CHIP COOKIES

½ cup sugar
½ cup brown sugar
⅓ cup butter, softened
⅓ cup shortening
1 egg
1 teaspoon vanilla
1½ cups sifted flour
½ teaspoon baking soda
Pinch of salt
½ cup chopped nuts or raisins
1 (6-ounce) package semisweet chocolate chips

Preheat the oven to 375 degrees F. Mix together the sugars, butter, shortening, egg, and vanilla. Stir in remaining ingredients. Drop the dough by rounded teaspoonfuls about 2 inches apart onto an ungreased cookie sheet. Bake until light brown, 8 to 10 minutes. Cool slightly before removing from cookie sheet. MAKES APPROXIMATELY 3½ DOZEN COOKIES.

RICE WITH CHOCOLATE MERINGUE

¼ cup well-washed rice
2 cups hot milk
Salt to taste
1 teaspoon butter
¼ cup sugar
¼ cup cocoa
½ cup cleaned seedless raisins
1 teaspoon vanilla
2 egg whites, beaten to stiff peaks
1 cup heavy cream, whipped to stiff peaks
Chocolate Meringue

Preheat oven to 350 degrees F. Cook the rice with the hot milk and a little salt in the top of a double boiler. When the rice is cooked, add the butter, sugar, cocoa, raisins, and vanilla. Fold the stiffly beaten egg whites and cream into the batter. Then pour the rice mixture into a buttered pudding dish, cover it with Chocolate Meringue, and brown the top in a moderate oven. SERVES 4 TO 6.

CHOCOLATE MERINGUE

4 egg whites, beaten to stiff peaks
6 tablespoons powdered sugar
6 teaspoons cocoa

Preheat oven to 350 degrees F. Stir into the egg whites, the powdered sugar and cocoa. Mix them together well.

VIII.
THE ULTIMATE FEAST
THAT NEVER WAS

IN THE AUTUMN OF HER IMPLAUSIBLE LIFE, AIMEE CROCKER, SOCIETY'S poor-little-rich-girl and heiress to a famous fortune, decided to tell nearly "all" in a potentially scandalous autobiography. This improbable project understandably stunned the *haute monde* of her Nob Hill *coterie*. Those aging belles, who had mostly survived their husbands *and* the vicissitudes of time, were terrified that the undaunted scribbler might reveal some carefully hidden "unpleasant" secrets. As it turned out, the venerable belles worried in vain. The unfettered object of their dread had been married too many times herself, and she had left behind too many identifiable lovers, to waste space in her chronicles on anybody *but* herself.

Aimee Crocker burst upon the unsuspecting world somewhere in the vicinity of sedate Sacramento. She was not pretty, but she grew up believing she would cease to be "A prisoner of biology and history . . ." and surely bloom to become a stunner. And to everyone's astonishment but her own, at age fifteen, she did. From that time on, her life was to be a series of louche sensual lunges, experienced to the fullest and remarkably free of guilt. "I was not immoral," she later stated in her book, "but *a*moral. I have lived fully and richly and I thank God for it!"

At about this time, her mother decided her little girl should be "finished" in a properly exclusive school, so Aimee was admitted to such an institution. Little did the corseted headmistress realize that she had loosed an Alexandrine nymphet in her virginal premises. Bored to death by her restricted school life in Sacramento, Aimee pressured her family until she was allowed to go on a supposedly chaperoned tour of the capitals of Europe. Still in her teens, she found the effete paleness of the Etonian "bloods" much to her liking, but she really struck pay dirt when she succumbed to the dubious charms of an Andalusian bullfighter with the prosaic name of Miguel. Her unmistakable ardor for this dark athlete so alarmed her traveling guardians that she was immediately rushed home to San Francisco

MADAME AIMEE CROCKER GOURAUD
Photo courtesy of the California Section, California State Library

to be thrown into the safe and sane arms of her first husband-to-be, Porter Ashe, a jolly innocent and a scion of an old, rich, dignified Northern California family.

The new Mrs. Ashe unfortunately found her husband a somewhat normal man, inadequate to match her fiery nature. The couple soon divorced. Aimee then headed off to begin her unrestricted life. Many years and miles later, having spent oodles of money, the millionairess became the Princess Galitzine. This Russian title was quite freely up for grabs until she acquired it with as much ease as needed to purchase a new bauble. Before becoming Russianized, she had been the companion of a Japanese baron, the mistress of a Hong Kong brigand, the lover of a Rumanian actor, and a playmate to a rugged individual in the humid jungles of Borneo. Through these melodramatic, fetid, and often poignant episodes, perhaps she had married— or perhaps she hadn't. Although she surely must have felt occasionally disenchanted or disappointed with the men in her life, Aimee always insisted that she remained "pure at heart."

Even San Franciscans, always ready to smile at most human transgressions, were startled by one of her most lurid adventures. High society shuddered when it was reported that the bemused, madcap heiress had "adopted" a four-foot-long boa constrictor. She had "met" the monster while traveling in Asia, and she, thereafter, insisted that the unique pet travel with her because its touch was "sensuous" to her skin. . . .

Aimee Crocker was at home in San Francisco during 1915, the year of the glorious Panama-Pacific Exposition. The glamour of the event obviously appealed to her romantic nature. Never known to hide from the spotlight, Aimee attracted national attention when she advertised that she would pay many thousands to any person who suggested the most imaginative banquet to be staged at the exposition. She had not bothered to ask permission to mount this extravaganza, so, naturally, the advertisement sparked an imbroglio with the exposition managers. The lady herself was Madame Gouraud at the time, but she believed she had the invincible power Reginald Turner gave his fictional heroine, the Princess Aldobranfalconiere. Aimee described herself as feeling "inspired by an unknown divinity . . ." to make the astonishing offer.

Joseph Charles Lehner, a San Francisco writer, publisher, and self-styled "American Gastronome," responded to Aimee Crocker's challenge with stupendous flair. In a book he published himself, he outlined an entire banquet *à la grand concours*. In Lehner, the heiress had finally found a free spirit that, like her own, was compounded by a true sense of the fantastic.

JOSEPH LEHNER'S
Le Grand Dîner au Natural à la Grand Concours

Setting:
A crystal pavilion of glass, *à la mode de Caen,* set amid verdant Amazonian gardens and lit by a facsimile of the fullest moon of the year. At the edge of the gardens, rows of blooming century plants.

Service:
The "Court of Gastronomic Delights" is tended by table servants in immaculate livery. Bewigged, of course.

Special Effects:
In the pavilion, a revolving stage is mounted. As it slowly turns, it passes through curtains that effect changes of the *tableaux vivants.*

Prelude:
Paderewski plays Chopin sonatas on the moving platform during the service of cocktails.

Hors d'oeuvre:
Crocodile eggs with caviar dressing, personally prepared by Escoffier himself. African Hottentots perform native dances of the wildest frenzy and abandon.

The Soup:
Soup Tortuga, served on the backs of living Galápagos Island turtles. Mary Garden sings a special adaptation of the Meditation from *Thaïs,* with violin obbligato.

The Fish:
Freshwater trout, shipped from the cold streams of Europe. Other water creatures are displayed in giant aquariums on the stage. Tyrolean singers and dancers yodel and execute charming clogs.

The Choice Entrées:

Preceded by a trumpet fanfare, Monkey Stew and Bear Steaks. Four live bears appear on stage with tree monkeys riding on their backs.

The Pièce de Résistance:

Tiger Roast. The service is accompanied by the entire membership of the John Philip Sousa band playing *La Marseillaise*. A live Bengal tiger is displayed on the stage.

The Dessert:

Peach Melba. Madame Nellie Melba sings the entire Mad Scene from *Lucia di Lammermoor*.

Interlude:

As Madame Melba disappears behind the curtain, the garden's aspect is transformed to that of a lush oasis, the "Court of a Thousand Flames."

Demitasse:

The richest Turkish coffee. The waiters pass among the palms with blazing torches. A theatrical group dressed as dangerous Mamelukes in dashing native costumes whirl like dervishes on the platform.

Conclusion:

Twelve Japanese Geisha girls immediately move among the guests, acting as natural fans. Parisian Tangos are played by the Cannes Society orchestra.

One wonders why Joseph Charles Lehner did not include Aimee Crocker's own electrifying snake dance in the list of entertainment—perhaps the gentleman believed the attraction would distract from the elegance and *politesse* of the occasion: It seems a great pity, however, that San Francisco would have been denied the same exotic treat that had amazed the cream of Europe's society while it slurped up the booze at the exclusive drinking troughs of Cap d'Antibes. . . .

Of course, Aimee Crocker's ultimate feast was never staged, and there is no record to prove that Lehner received the prize money. We can be thankful that nobody has ever dared or attempted to present a blasphemously diluted version of this lunatic extravaganza. But it is delightful to fantasize about how perfectly Aimee Crocker's sumptuous dinner would have brought the gaslight days to an end in San Francisco: A grand finale by a gilded girl from a golden era in a glittering town.

GENERAL INDEX

RECIPE INDEX

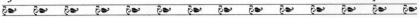